Surviving Suicide

DATE DUE			

Praise for
Surviving Suicide:
My Journey to the Light Within

Surviving Suicide: My Journey to the Light Within is really a book about going from pain and grief that seems impossible to deal with to the Peace of God. It is a courageous book written from the depth of the heart and soul. **Dr. Gerald G. Jampolsky**, M.D., bestselling author of several books including *Love is Letting Go of Fear.*

Both a disturbing and an inspirational book. Mary Scovel's description of the mental illness and suicide of her two sons, of her struggle through the stages of grief, and of her journey to spiritual awakening, was a life changing experience for me. She has opened her heart and shared her story in a way that will draw the reader into an intimate relationship with her, as you feel her devastation and pain, and finally, the joy of her understanding of the meaning of power that is the Highest Power within us all. **Dr. Mary M. Polite**, Professor, Southern Illinois University Edwardsville.

Your book offers hope to survivors and their marriages. **Marian Nadybal**, Suicide Prevention Action Network (SPAN USA)

Losing one of my sons to suicide was the single worst horrible experience of my life. As Mary Scovel shared her devastation and search for answers after the loss of both of her sons, I was comforted in knowing I was not alone in many of the feelings that surface after the suicide of a loved one. Mary's path to healing and peace of mind will truly be an inspiration to other suicide survivors, wherever they may be on their individual journeys. **Ethel Bucek**, R.N., B.A., facilitator, West Michigan Survivors of Suicide.

It was only after reading this book that my husband and I found courage to share our feelings with each other after our twin sons' suicides. In identifying with other parents who had this grave loss, this book freed us to communicate our sorrow and heartache with one another. **Marge Huck**, Hilton Head Island Survivor of Suicide Support Group.

The sorrow of losing your children knows no boundaries—it's an unknown journey. Mary Scovel takes our hand and gently guides us through this journey with authenticity, insight and warmth. This is an extraordinary book about trauma and love, about life. Reading this book makes us all a little more human. **Andrea Farbman**, Ed.D., CEO of American Music Therapy Association.

As I read this tremendously touching and sorrowful story, I was struck by the courage and ultimately, the powerful belief in family and life. In this unimaginable experience, I could feel the pain of loss, the probing for answers, and the eventual attainment of spiritual serenity. This is a powerful, loving and helpful book on suicide and family healing. **Joyce Darcangelo**, T & S, OHNC, RN Psychiatric Nurse.

Surviving Suicide: My Journey to the Light Within is a remarkable, candid and courageous recounting of Mary's journey following her sons' deaths. It is the story of her battle with indescribable pain and doubt and her gradual spiritual awakening to insight, wisdom and healing found within. This book will be helpful to and treasured by all those who sit in darkness and yearn for the light. **Rev. Dr. Lynn A. DeMoss**, United Methodist Church.

It has been said that what we choose not to look at will rule our lives. What fear, that we dare not behold, holds sway in our lives? This book illuminates the darkest recesses of our deepest fears. It is a book for those who are willing to peer into the shadows and face the worst a parent can imagine: the self-destruction of a beloved child is not a journey for the faint of heart, but one for those who dare to ask that their hearts be broken open. It is a story of incredible suffering and courage, a story that will make you cry. You may find, as I did, that your tears will wash away stiffness in your body; that you may discover in Mary's love and courage something of your own, some realization of the sweetness of this moment and all the beauty that fills it. **Mary Westmoreland**.

Walking hand in hand with Mary on her dark journey has given me the courage to finally face my own healing path. **Rosanne Ball**.

As a facilitator of grief support groups for hospice, I listen to many personal journeys through grief. As I come to know their stories of life and love, I hear the profound sense of loss that is felt from the survivors. This is how I have come to know of the Scovels' horrific experience of the death of two sons by suicide. Mary's book is a wonderful memoir of love and dedication. It honors her role as a wife and as a mother who survives and transcends the depths of this tragedy. It takes the reader through a very personal world where mental illness, death, tragedy, grieving, hope, faith and healing are explored and shared. For those experiencing this loss, it is enormously helpful to hear from one who has been there, and who brings back a story of managing to find peace and joy in living life. **Renee Pigat**, MPH Bereavement Coordinator Hospice Care of the Lowcountry.

As a psychotherapist I use Mary's book in working with clients who share a similar painful loss. Survivors of suicide have struggled in silence due to the stigma placed on them by society, and now by reading this book they have someone who understands their grief. I recommend this book for anyone experiencing such a loss. **Linda Boyd**, L.I.S.W., Psychiatric Social Worker.

For Ward,

the love of my life who makes my soul sing

Contents

Acknowledgements

First of all, I want to thank my husband, Ward, for his love and patience and being my cheerleader in seeing this book come to fruition.

For their on-going encouragement, I also thank my daughters and sons-in-law, Marcia and Tom Sprague and Kathy and Richard Rodrigue.

I wish to thank my first reader and editor, Cheryl Niggle for her unceasing belief in me. I thank Jo Williams, for her excellent editing critiques and her willingness to share her knowledge of the publishing process with me.

I would also like to express my profound gratitude to my dear friend, Mary Polite for her patience and her invaluable input and advice in reorganizing and rephrasing major sections of this book.

I am especially grateful to Kathy Wall, my friend and three-time author whose sensitivity and objectivity in revising and completing the final editing process is invaluable.

And to Jerry Jampolsky, who in his great capacity to love, believed in the message of this book, early on.

I feel so fortunate to have such a loving circle of friends. I thank them for being advisors as this book and I evolved. I thank Barbara Conn, Valerie Farra, Marge Huck, Jen and Dave Lyle, Beryl Title, Dr. Lynn DeMoss, Chris Bohn, Lorraine deBaptiste, Dick and Marion DeVinney, Jean McMannus, Michael Shapiro, Don Bremer, Barbara Harris, my brother in-law, Don Scovel, my brother, David Sennema and my sister-in-law, Marty Sennema, and my sister, Carol Derks and brother-in-law, Harold Derks for their love and assistance.

I appreciate my friends, Rosanne Ball, Linda Boyd, Michelle Chambers, Marita Collins and Mary Westmoreland for their insights and enthusiasm.

I thank Joyce Darcangelo, Debbie Rankin, Andi Farbman, Elizabeth St. Angelo, and Suzanne Wright for their unconditional love.

For all those who know the pain of losing loved ones to suicide, I thank all my friends in SOS groups for their compassion and understanding and Renee Pigat, Jerry and Elsie Weyrauch, Ethel Bucek, and Marian Nadybal for their support.

13

I also acknowledge Elke Neubeuer, Rich Lucas, Carol Tietjan and Catherine Bower for holding up this vision in prayer.

Special thanks to my dear musician friends, David Bohn and Charlie McCracken, for accompanying my song, "My Broken Heart" and for being there for me in the recording of my CD.

And to my dear friend, Margaret Pratt and her son Ryan J. Pratt, many thanks for their love and vision in designing the cover of my book.

I'm grateful to all those who let me use their names and their stories and to all my friends and family for their support and encouragement.

Best of all, I send my appreciation to George Trask, a man of integrity, for the quality work accomplished by Coastal Villages Press.

Surviving Suicide

Steve and Carl, best of friends, 1983.

1

My Heart is Broken

"The Darkness Has No Power over the Light."[1]

Ernest Holmes

My story

My heart is broken. I didn't know how I'd live without Steve and Carl, but I've had to learn since Steve's death in 1988 and Carl's in 1993. Both of my sons suffered with schizophrenia, and both took their own lives. Each day I move a little farther out of the personal hell created by the devastating loss of Steve at the age of twenty-seven and Carl, who was thirty, because I have taken a spiritual journey. Each day the Light within becomes brighter as I continue on my personal quest towards peace. The "short of it" is that the path has taken me through the typical stages of grief: denial, anger, bargaining, depression, and acceptance. The "long of it" is that total surrender lies beyond acceptance, and mine is a lifetime process. My choice in seeking total transformation means that I give over completely to Spirit, who has been and continues to be my Light within.

Any parent who has buried a child understands the depth of devastation, unbearable to describe. Any parent who has faced that experience with the knowledge that her child's death was chosen by his own hand knows an ache beyond the intolerable. My own pain was further deepened in grappling with and trying to understand mental illness, the diagnosis of schizophrenia, and a mental health system designed to provide support which failed miserably in that attempt.

But I can't tell the story of any parent. I can only tell my own.

Facing Ward, my husband of forty-six years, at the moment when he told me our oldest son, Steve, had committed suicide was the darkest day of my life. I could not believe what he was saying. I just could not believe. I wanted to run and see for myself, but I chose not to witness the horror of my son hanging from the rafters in the basement. Somehow, if I didn't set eyes on him, maybe it wouldn't be true. I was convinced this was only a bad dream as I watched the coroner take the body bag away. Nothing was ever the same again.

I never thought for a moment that Steve would end his own life. But it was true: my Steve was dead.

We called Carl and our daughters, Marcia and Kathy, then married and living out of state, with the horrible news. We all wept in disbelief.

The stress of burying our son challenged us in ways we'd never dreamed. In the scheme of life, of rearing a family, the early death of a child is unnatural, untimely, and unexpected. When a child takes his own life, the grief and shame are exacerbated by a society which lays its judgment on the family.

It was comforting to have our three children with us. We talked and cried into the wee hours of the night about what had happened to Steve and why he might have done this, why he hadn't come to us for help, how much we would miss him, and how our family would never be the same again. After awhile, Carl began sharing some funny stories about Steve, and soon we were all talking about our happy memories.

After the funeral, however, no one spoke Steve's name to us. Not only were our church friends silent, but so were our extended family members. I tried to think of why this alienation was happening. Perhaps our congregation was in shock that a pastor's son could take his life. Perhaps his act forced people to look at their own mortality, adding to their discomfort. Perhaps, too, people become unnerved when hearing about the loss of a child because they don't want to acknowledge that it could happen in their family as well. And perhaps my family was afraid I would be upset and cry if they talked about Steve.

Ward and I, along with our three children, were alone to grieve, process, and accept Steve's death. I never felt such despair before in my life. I walked around in a daze, preoccupied with my own feelings of self-pity and hurt. There were times I didn't think the agonizing pain would ever go away. A poignant passage about suicide I had read somewhere along the way kept coming to mind: "It was like you have a social disease. No one wants to talk about it but they wonder where you caught it and what you did to your kid." The silence was deafening.

Ward and I retreated to our cottage where we shut out the world, wanting only to be with each other. We read books, cried separately and together, and held each other closely. We talked about all the happy memories we shared with Steve, as well as the angry words that had passed between us, and the control issues that fed our guilt. One of my favorite havens was the wooden swing located on the patio facing the lake. As the rhythmic motion lulled me back and forth, I felt a calmness come over me. Looking out at the beautiful, clear blue sky and seeing the gentle movement of the sailboat in the sparkling water, I was mesmerized temporarily as I moved beyond my own small world of pain.

Little did I know that five years later I would reconnect with that ache in my soul that I so wanted to leave behind.

June 18, 1993. That date will forever live in my memory. Carl's case manager came to our house that day to give us the news of Carl's death. Following in the footsteps of his older brother, Carl had hanged himself.

I was plunged back into horrendous grief once again, this time for the loss of my younger son.

At the committal service, Carl's ashes were interred in Steve's grave. Although the box was small and placed above Steve's casket, my feeling of profound loss returned with a vengeance, not just for Carl, but again for Steve. My sister stood behind me and put her hands on my shoulders in a gesture of comfort that helped to calm me.

When Steve took his life and then, five years later, his younger brother, Carl, followed suit, I closely examined every guilty feeling I harbored. Despite my internal dialogue, the questions and doubts persisted. *Why would a tragedy like this happen to our family? Why did they do this to themselves? Why would they do this to us? What did I do or say to cause them to do this? What didn't I do that would have made a difference? How could have I prevented this?* I looked for places to lay blame: my sons, the mental health system, the hospitals, insensitive people, the church, God, and of course, myself.

My healing finally began as I wrestled with these questions. I started to see life from an alternative perspective. I realized we are all responsible for ourselves. Steve's and Carl's actions were not my fault, nor Ward's. No parent is responsible for what his or her child does as an adult. I accepted I had been a good parent, doing everything I knew how to love and support our children. Carl and Steve, in those last moments before their deaths, much to my dismay, made their own decisions to end their suffering.

The pain of my sons' suicides was so unbearable that Ward and I truly believed that "starting over" would be healing for both of us. I resigned from my job as a professor of music therapy, a career I had enjoyed for twenty-five years. Ward vacated his pastorate of twenty-two years from the United Methodist Church. Having been married nearly four decades and having spent all of that time in the state of Michigan, we left for Oklahoma where Ward would be on staff at a seminary and I would be a director of music. After building our dream house in a "spiritual community," we lived there only two years. On the road again, we found our way to Arkansas, eventually buying a home overlooking a beautiful lake in the Ozarks. After another two years, though, we sold everything and moved to Hawaii, where we stayed for almost twenty four months. Presently we are living on Hilton Head Island, South Carolina.

This is the story of my family and the journey we have taken to find the center of peace which finally supported the writing of this book. Although I have often felt alone in dealing with loss, I know there are others who have suffered as well. I am hopeful that this book will be an inspiration to those who live with mental illness, the stigma of suicide, or the loss of family members to embark as I have on a spiritual journey inward which leads from pain to peace, and finally to the Light within.

2

Family Portraits

"Trust in the Divine Plan, bless it and bless the Divine Order
inherent in every person and every situation."[1]

Shanta Kelly Hartzel

My growing years

I received a thunderous applause the night I was born. I was welcomed lovingly into this world on a cold winter night in January at home in Grand Rapids, Michigan, by my paternal grandmother and her sister who were there assisting the female obstetrician at my birth. My four year-old sister and eighteen month-old brother were staying overnight with relatives. My father wasn't home either. I was born while he accompanied the prestigious men's chorus, the Schubert Club. Toward the end of the concert, the president of the club announced that Carl Sennema had a new baby daughter, and the audience applauded my arrival. Symbolically, it was the universe greeting me and telling me I had a great gift to bring to this earth; and, like my father, that gift turned out to be my music.

Growing up in my family, I had no outlet for my feelings except through my music. There was no open exchange of how we felt and no room for anything but perfection, an impossible expectation. Very early in life, I began to hide my feelings because expressing them only caused me pain. I felt as if I were wearing Harry Potter's cloak of invisibility, and no one saw me or listened to me. I remember our mealtimes as being devoid of any conversation and recall a few times feeling confused and sad as I observed my dad crying. I knew I belonged to this family but never felt accepted for who I was. I longed for someone to talk to me. I felt very lonely and drifted along like a ship without a sail.

Security is manifested in strange ways. When I reached sixth grade, I remember being embarrassed that I weighed more than my girlfriends. My brother teased me, and I had no tools to express my rage and despair. So I stuffed all of my feelings inside and took on everyone else's pain and suffering. I thought I was to blame for it all. I went into denial and pretended nothing was wrong with my family. I found my safety in being quiet, keeping busy, and obeying my parents so I wouldn't shame them. At some point along the way, though, I became aware of my own inner strength which allowed me to overcome some of this personal pain.

My soul sings when I create music. I was happiest when I could read the intricate line of harmony while singing in the children's church choir directed by my dad. Practicing scales and études gave me a command of the piano, and I learned the finger techniques easily. Taking lessons from my dad, however, was both a challenge and a joy. He was nurturing, yet moody, and I felt as if I would never measure up to his expectations. I loved our church's majestic pipe organ which he taught me to play in high school. So I immersed myself in music, knowing at some level that my self-worth was tied up in this accomplishment. In junior high school the director of the orchestra needed a double bass player, so the deep bass sound of strings thundered with the push and pull of my bow. Becoming bored with that instrument after two years, I played clarinet in the high school orchestra, took voice lessons, and sang in the school chorus. My music ability paid off when I helped my girlfriend get through chorus while she helped me through chemistry class.

I don't know when my dad began to drink heavily, but it was obvious that this was a family secret I was not to tell anyone. At age twelve, I recall boarding a bus and riding a long distance with my mother to a private psychiatric hospital to visit my dad. I was told he "needed a rest from his job," but I didn't understand the impact of that information at the time. When I saw him I felt sad. Years later, after my dad died at a young age of fifty-seven, my mother agreed to sign forms for the release of information from the facility where he had been hospitalized. I read the sketchy medical documentation and could only surmise that he had been admitted for depression.

Between ages six and sixteen, I had three medical emergencies: tonsillectomy, appendectomy, and swollen glands. My body was definitely giving me strong messages about my frozen emotional state; but, at the time, I didn't understand there was any connection.

I loved high school. I focused on my relationships with my friends and my music as my means of survival and building self-worth. Besides my involvement in music, I enjoyed the camaraderie of the synchronized swimming team and the excitement of cheerleading.

The love of my life

I met the love of my life, Ward, in eighth grade at a pizza party after a football game. From our first encounter I knew he was special. We talked about everything. He listened to me and loved me for who I was. We were immediately drawn together and dated throughout high school.

However, I might never have met Ward if the well known Coats and Clark Thread Company hadn't transferred his father from his sales position in Chicago, where Ward was born, to Grand Rapids, Michigan, when Ward was twelve years old.

When he was four, his brother, Don, was born. Soon after his baby brother arrived, Ward developed an ear infection which settled in his left hip as osteomyelitis. After the doctors put him in a body cast, he was immobile and spent many hours sitting in the back yard with his best companion, his mutt dog, Rusty. He and Rusty would watch the neighborhood kids play games. He also spent some time getting acquainted with his new baby brother when his mother would spread out a blanket and let the boys play together. Although his hip healed, it was weakened due to the bones becoming honeycombed, but it didn't keep this curious and adventurous little boy from being very active.

Before he moved to Michigan, he attended a strict Lutheran school in a Chicago suburb. He made new friends quickly in Michigan when he joined the sixth grade football team. Even though doctors had advised him not to play football because of his weakened hip, it was his favorite team sport, and he was not to be dissuaded. In high school he was the fastest guard on the team for the first five yards, and he became captain of the football team.

The junior college we attended was in the same town as our high school. But after one year, Ward, tired of school, accepted a job with Coats and Clark. The company's headquarters was located in Skokie, Illinois; so, at age nineteen, he packed his bags and moved to the Chicago area where he was assigned the Wisconsin, Iowa and Illinois districts.

He liked his job as a salesman; but, after traveling for a year, staying in hotels, and being alone, he proposed. As a newly married couple, we moved in the summer of 1956 to Rockford, Illinois.

While Ward was a salesman for Coats and Clark, his territory included three states, which required excessive travel. He left on Sunday evening and returned home late Friday afternoon. Although we attended church and made a new circle of friends, being on the road during the week took its toll as he didn't have much time to spend with his family or himself. He struggled in his religious understanding and doubted the presence of God's love in his life.

One evening, driving along the highway to Iowa, he felt such despair that he asked, "God, if you love me, give me a sign so I might know your presence in my life." Suddenly he saw lightning strike off in the distant sky. He was curious but unconvinced. So he said once more, "God, if you really love me, you'll give me another sign when I count to ten." He slowly counted to ten and waited, doubting this time that anything would happen. Then, he saw a huge bolt of lightening up in the dark sky. Still a doubting Thomas, he said again, "God, if you really love me, show me one more time after I count to ten." The final number was barely out of his mouth when lightning struck again, and the sky lit up before him. He was so overwhelmed with joy that he began sobbing and shaking uncontrollably. Finally he drove his car off onto the shoulder of the road. He thanked God for answering his prayer. Feeling totally grateful but

Ward and Mary as an engaged couple, 1955.

humbled, he turned the car around and came back home to tell me the good news. This was the beginning of his spiritual journey.

After Ward had been working for Coats and Clark for five years, we moved back to Michigan. Wanting to complete his college training, he was motivated to take evening classes to finish his bachelor's degree. Achieving an "A" in a course on logic would be the criterion for continuing his college education. That accomplished, he then took a sociology course and signed up for a project for extra credit. This venture, which opened up an opportunity to work as a chaplain in a nearby jail with inmates, was so life changing, he decided to switch careers at age thirty-eight, get his master's of divinity degree and enter the United Methodist ministry.

Five years into his ministerial career he was overwhelmed with pain from his hip. The doctors suggested waiting as long as possible before surgery, but he needed an exorbitant amount of medication to give him relief from the pain. Surgery was scheduled. The doctor put the longest possible prosthesis in his hip, hoping that his left leg would be the same length as his right, but the bone was collapsing in on itself and had atrophied. The operation was successful in that he no longer had any physical pain, but he would soon experience a deep ache of another kind.

When our sons died, he wept bitterly and suffered the agonizing pain of the profound and unbelievable loss of a loving father. Because of this loss he sought therapy. During that time he also experienced a life-altering, near-death experience. Through it all, Ward has continued to be a spiritual seeker.

Our family

Thirteen months into our marriage, we began our family. Our four children were born approximately two years apart: Marcia, 1957; Kathy; 1959, Steve; 1961 and Carl, 1963.

Our first child

Marcia Lynn was born when I was a young twenty-one year-old, excited to be a mom. I was overjoyed as I held my daughter lovingly and felt her tiny hand around my finger. I remember feeling tremendous love and awe as I looked into her soft blue eyes and said, "I am your mother, and you are my precious daughter, Marcia."

Of course, everything she did was a new experience for Ward and me, and we reveled in her every accomplishment, her first step, her first word. She was only three when we took her to the hospital to have her tonsils and adenoids removed. She was so tiny but so brave as they wheeled her away hugging her favorite, fuzzy, red, kewpie doll.

Before we knew it she was learning to ride a two-wheeled bike, to swim, to play piano and violin, and water-ski. In high school she found her talent and love for writing stories and poetry. She played violin and competed for first chair in the high school orchestra for four years. Marcia also played violin in the youth symphony and won a scholarship to Interlochen, a music summer camp. At the university she majored in sociology, minored in music and psychology, and worked in the library to earn spending money.

A few weeks after her college graduation, she traveled to Africa where she served in the Peace Corps for two years. She wrote a letter home tell-

Steve, Marcia, Carl, Kathy, Christmas 1963.

ing us of her first moments in a village in Sierra Leone. She was dropped off and found herself standing alone in the middle of the downtown square, so she took out her ukulele and began to play. The children began walking towards her, curious about this new "stranger" in their midst. After two years in the Peace Corp, she returned home to Michigan and worked as a mental health professional.

She married and moved to the east coast where she became a licensed massage therapist. Several years after her divorce, she remarried. She and Tom have two daughters, Kayla and Devi. Marcia is teaching music in the public schools, gives private violin lessons, fiddles, snowshoes, and is on a spiritual quest.

Our second daughter

We were so happy when Katherine Ann was born March 6, 1959, seventeen months after Marcia. Kathy had big brown eyes and wavy brown hair. As I held her I realized how blessed I was to have another beautiful daughter. I sang to her and told her how special she was. She walked and talked at an early age, a natural development to be able to catch up and communicate with her sister. She and Marcia were inseparable friends and playmates.

At an early age, Kathy loved to act. We called her our "Sara Bernhardt." She was our free spirit. While Marcia followed the rules, Kathy rebelled against them. As she grew up, she took ballet lessons, loved to water ski, reluctantly played piano and become an actress in the school plays.

The first time she picked up a flute she made a full and rich sound, and her vibrato came easily. In the orchestra she was assigned to the first chair of the flute section. When "try-outs" came around, she decided not to show up, so she was re-assigned to the fourteenth chair. I was upset at her irresponsibility, but she explained that she wanted to sit and talk with her friend in the back row rather than stay in the leadership position.

When she was in tenth grade we moved to Eaton, Ohio, where she played flute in the marching band. One rainy evening she marched along with other band members and went through the motions of playing, having lost the end of her flute somewhere on the football field.

Her first year at a traditional university she accomplished her goal to be on the Dean's List. Her second year, she transferred to a college that was more unconventional, thrived in her studies, and earned her master's degree in psychology. Her summers were spent in Alaska where she worked in the fish canneries to earn money for college. She and her husband, Richard, have a son, Dylan. Presently Kathy is teaching music in an elementary school, gives flute lessons and is the school's fundraiser.

Our sons

It seems only a short time ago when, in 1961, I held my newborn son, Steven Ward, in my arms. As I caressed his soft, pink skin, I marveled at how perfect he was. I was overwhelmed with joy and gratitude to have an eight pound, four ounce, healthy baby boy. Looking into his dark blue eyes, I knew they would soon become deep brown like his sister Kathy's and mine. When the day finally came to take him home from the hospital, I dressed him in a soft, yellow shirt that had a cute little duck embroidered on the front. It was a beautiful sunny day, but to protect him from the warm wind I wrapped him in a light blue quilt with dancing white lambs that would soon be his favorite. His two sisters, Marcia and Kathy, were anxiously waiting at the door to greet their new brother. They each held out their arms and begged to hold him. Steve was very content to have them hug and kiss him and take him for long rides in the buggy.

Even from the first, Steve was as musical as Mozart. Music seemed to be his destiny. He showed his gifts very early on. At the young age of two, sitting in the car seat next to me, we would sing "Jesus Loves Me." As I listened to his soft, lilting voice, my heart leapt with joy at his sweet song of pure love. While growing up, Steve was always playing a tune on an instrument, humming, whistling, or singing. He moved quickly from the recorder to the cornet, finally falling in love with the trumpet. He also taught himself to play the piano and the guitar.

He was a healthy and handsome boy who never gave us a day of worry.

Just before Steve's second birthday, a new baby brother, Carl, came into his life. Right from the beginning the boys were inseparable, both each other's best ally and staunchest opponent. While playing for hours with G.I. Joe dolls, Legos, and innumerable games, I could hear them arguing one minute and laughing gut-wrenching giggles the next.

Carl never wanted to miss anything. He even arrived prematurely. When my water broke seven weeks before my due date my doctor gave me many mixed messages about what to expect with a premature birth. He warned me that the baby might not make it. But one week later I was in awe as my baby's head crowned and all four pounds, eight ounces of him came into this world. His hearty cry brought me tears of joy and re-lief. I held him closely before the nurses hurriedly took him to the incu-bator, which would be his home for the next, long, four weeks.

After he finally reached five pounds and we were able to bring him home, I would often lay Carl gently across Steve's lap and watch Steve hug and kiss his baby brother, asking when he was going to be big enough for him to play with. The moment Carl could sit up by himself, Marcia, age six, and Kathy, age four, pulled their brothers in the red wagon and took them for many walks around the neighborhood.

Carl and Steve, buddies, 1968.

At an early age Carl demonstrated a remarkable ability to draw three-dimensional pictures. In kindergarten, he did a drawing of a horse that was extremely detailed. He also went through a phase of making noises instead of speaking to us. At the time we laughed because it sounded so silly, but we encouraged him to use words to express himself. Eventually he found other ways to gain our attention.

Rearing our children

While Ward and I were rearing our children, we both worked outside the home. I hold degrees in Music Education and Music Therapy, while Ward earned a degree in Philosophy, a Masters of Divinity, and a Ph.D. I began my career as professor of music education, then worked as a music therapist in clinical settings, after which I became a professor of music therapy. After leaving his sales job, Ward served the United Methodist Church for twenty-two years.

Some of our happiest times together as a family were spent at our cottage. Ward and I owned a summer place only thirty-five miles north of our home so I could pack up and be there quickly. Our cottage was located on a beautiful 1000-acre lake. Nestled in among pine trees, it faced the west where I watched the gorgeous sunsets from the deck. Just walking into my "home away from home" I felt relaxed and carefree. I lived in the moment, leaving behind my busy schedules, job responsibilities, and city life.

Our summers were spent with friends and family. Water-skiing was our favorite pastime. While Ward drove the boat, I was the watcher in case anyone fell off the skis. The children competed as to who could make the biggest wake as they wove in and out on the slalom ski. When they double-skied I could see looks of joy and intensity on their faces as they ducked under each other's ropes, skiing across each other's wakes. Each summer, our children became more confident and more proficient. They reveled in showing off each new perfected trick. We all spent many hours teaching our friends and family, the youngest and the oldest, how to ski. Some learned fast while others never did get their balance well enough to enjoy a thrilling ride. Ward and the boys kept the gas tank filled, burning up at least 180 gallons of gas each summer. The boat was rarely idle.

Homemade ice cream was the popular dessert at the lake. I made up the wonderfully rich and creamy recipe, after which we'd decide what flavor we wanted that day. Should it be chocolate or vanilla or should we add fruit? The fun of making ice cream was for everyone to take a turn cranking the handle. The family rule was, if you want to eat, you take a turn cranking. When it finally became too hard to crank, we all watched with great anticipation as Ward took the top off the container. Was the ice cream hard? Was it ready to eat? The prize was a big dish of delicious homemade ice cream, so cold, it could give us a headache. Some smothered it with my home-made hot fudge topping and came back for seconds, while others enjoyed it plain.

Our cottage was a wonderful spot to gather, relax and socialize, a place that holds special memories of our young happy family.

Another important aspect of our family life was our love of music. Singing and playing musical instruments was a high priority, and all four of our children became proficient musicians. Marcia played violin, and Kathy chose the flute, while Steve loved his trumpet. Carl, at age four, began learning Suzuki violin. There was a continual flow of music in our home as I played piano for Marcia, Kathy and Steve for the numerous district and state music competitions they entered. I can still hum many of the melodies, since we practiced these pieces hundreds of times. I remember each of them nervously walking into a very quiet room where judges listened and rated their performance. I held my breath hoping they would play well under that pressure. There were tense moments at some of the competitions. When Kathy was asked to sight-read a piece of music, I could tell by the expression on her face that she wasn't sure how to count the rhythmic phrase. I wanted to leap up out of my chair and whisper in her ear, but she was on her own. For one of Marcia's violin performances for a music camp scholarship, in spite of our losing our place, she still received the scholarship and enjoyed her experiences at Interlochen Music Camp that summer. I also recall Steve's playing his heart out for three judges who sat there with no expression on their faces. I wondered how they could listen to a child play without giving him a smile of encouragement. As for Carl, most of his performances were with a group of twelve children learning to play the violin. Even though they were all motivated to practice, I was the taskmaster who often reminded them, "Have you practiced?" Or, "Let's play through your piece *now*."

As they became more proficient, Ward and I took our four children to perform for the poor and the powerless people who wouldn't otherwise have visitors. At the county jail, Ward led the inmates in the worship service. At the designated time, each of our children bravely stood up in front of this group of strangers to play his or her instrument. The minute the music started it seemed to calm and soothe the inmates as if angels were in the room. Those who had been agitated became mesmerized and listened attentively while not taking their eyes off the performer. The men were obviously touched by the music as they stood and gave our children a standing ovation.

Our family also entertained the patients at the psychiatric hospital where I worked. As we watched them amble into the room, they sat with us in a circle. The children began playing Christmas carols. I immediately noticed some smiles on their faces. I looked around the circle and saw one patient, who hadn't talked for a month, sing every word to the carols. The power of music was so magical in her life and in ours at that moment.

Participation in the extended family holiday music concert was a much anticipated yearly affair. Barbershop harmony, sung by my brother, his son and Steve and Carl touched our hearts. Then all the cousins, aunts, and uncles who could stand listening to the din of the rare combination of instruments joined in the playing and the laughter. While the young ones tried to get attention by playing their recorders, the older children and adults often drowned them out by playing flutes, violins, and trumpet, clarinet, piano and trombone. We promised each other we'd meet the following year to make another joyous memory.

Little did we know that our move to Ohio in 1975 would be the last time we would experience happy times together as a family. Our boys were in the prime of their lives and hadn't yet experienced mental illness.

Moving took a lot of preparation. Changes were set in motion. I quit my job at the university and looked toward finding employment in our new location. Our three youngest children would be enrolled in a new school and making new friends, while Marcia would begin her studies at a university 350 miles from us. I was leaving old friends and family, soon to become a rural dweller instead of an urban resident.

Moving day came quickly. As we drove away, I cried, looking back at the house we had called home for fourteen years, the house that held so many precious family memories. Our new life in Ohio seemed like only a dream.

Soon after Ward made his decision to attend seminary in Ohio, he inquired about serving a student church to gain pastoral experience and to have some income. The responsibilities included officiating at Sunday services and serving the congregation a few hours a week, a workable schedule for a busy seminary student. However, he was told there were no student churches available in the United Methodist Church near where he would attend seminary. Disappointed but determined, he talked to a person in the Placement Services who gave him the name of someone to call whose country church, located thirty-eight miles from seminary had requested a student pastor.

The policy of the church required that Ward be interviewed by a church committee and give one sermon, after which the church congregation would vote. We were all excited at the prospect of becoming the pastor's family for this church, and we offered to provide the music for the service where Ward would be preaching. We drove to Ohio for the Sunday morning service. Marcia and Kathy played a violin and flute duet, and Steve played his trumpet, then the children and I sang. We waited in great anticipation while the congregation voted. It was unanimous that we come. We were all thrilled.

My new home was a big, old, white farmhouse designated as the church parsonage, located on a 180-acre farm owned by a wonderful

Kathy, Ward, Mary, Marcia,
Carl, Steve, and our dog, Auggie, 1970.

family who lived next door. Their three children were similar in age to ours. Bill, the owner, greeted us cheerfully as we drove into the long driveway that led to the house.

"Welcome," he called out. "We're happy you're here."

He handed me a dozen eggs, "fresh from the barn," he promised, and chuckled as Steve and Carl made a dash for the barn to begin exploring this new phenomenon. Less than five minutes later, our Kathy was in deep conversation with her soon-to-be best friend, Susan.

After going to bed exhausted the first night, Ward and I were awakened by strange sounds outside. The next morning we looked across the road to discover the noise was pigpen lids flapping. I quickly learned about life down on the farm. Our friend, Bill, had a favorite saying when anything went wrong, which we readily adopted: "Life is tough on the farm."

Another aspect of country living taught me that, when the wind came from the east, I could expect a pungent smell drifting from the pig farm down the road. Also, the east wind meant the probability of a storm which, in the winter months, meant I had to park my car at the end of the driveway if I wanted to get to work the next day.

Since this was a student church and Ward's yearly salary was only $5,000, potlucks and the farmers' generous contributions from their fresh gardens were lifesavers for our family. I held four part-time jobs to help make ends meet. The engine of my VW "Bug" never had a chance to cool down as I traveled around Ohio teaching music at two universities and working two clinical music therapy jobs. Ward commuted thirty-eight miles to the United Theological Seminary and loved his classes. We were welcomed into this community with open arms and enjoyed our fellowship with the warm and friendly people in our "country" church.

At the first Sunday service, I soon realized that I was wearing a "new hat" as I heard someone remark, "That's the minister's wife." I liked the sound of it and soon became involved in people's lives as well as singing in the choir and filling in as organist when needed.

Living on the farm for three years was like looking in a kaleidoscope where I saw new shapes and colors everywhere. I savored our life there which brought a new perspective and new experiences that city life could never offer.

Then we moved back to the city and our life changed forever.

3

Steve's Loving Song

"I sit high and I sight the Joel when I feel I have the strength."
Steven W. Scovel

You have a son!

When I heard the words, "You have a boy," and I heard Steve's first cry, I was ecstatic. "We have a son, Ward, we have a son!" I exclaimed. "What a great gift! I am so happy."
And he was an adorable child, good-natured and content.

Naptime came easily for Steve. I would find him in the most unusual places lying asleep on the floor, dressed in his favorite Buster Brown sweater, his thumb in his mouth and his favorite blanket closely hugging his body. He was so cute and cuddly. He went through a stage where, no matter what the temperature, he would cry until I found his most-wanted sweater.

Steve loved to dress up in Halloween costumes. He took such pride in his blue, red and silver Captain Marvel suit I made for him. To complete his outfit he painted the garbage can lid a bright blue and, grinning from ear to ear, held the "shield" out in front of him for all to see.

Like all first-graders, he decided to play T-ball with his school friends. We never missed a game, and we watched him standing in the outfield playing with the stones and sand at his feet, totally oblivious to the ball coming his way. However, when it came time for him to learn how to ride a bike, he eagerly jumped on his new reddish-orange two-wheeler. After a shaky start getting his balance, he caught on quickly and rode away down the street with ease.

When he was six years old, he auditioned for a TV program. The producer was so taken with Steve's charisma and charm that out of 200 children auditioning, Steve was selected for the popular, local children's program. He, along with a little girl, were the two leading actors. We all gathered around the TV set every Saturday morning for six months and watched his star performance. He was a happy child and loved his family.

At ten years old Steve had a beautiful and pure soprano voice. The choir director at church cast him as Amahl in the opera, *Amahl and the Night Visitors,* and I was chosen as Amahl's mother. Steve and I memorized our lines and practiced our songs together. I was astonished, yet pleased at how easily he learned the difficult music. The night of the performance, just before curtain time, Steve and I peeked out to see who was in the audience. It took my breath away to see our church sanctuary filled, even the second balcony.

"There must be a thousand people out there," I said nervously. Steve and I looked at each other and acknowledged anxious delight at seeing this huge crowd of people. He put on a stellar performance.

He was a "ham," and he had a special way of engaging the audience when he performed. His impersonation of Elvis Presley brought the house down at a talent show held in the social hall of our church. Steve was definitely in his element as he sang into the microphone, swayed back and forth, and belted out, "You ain't nothin' but a hound dog." He gave a bow as he received a standing ovation.

He seemed to be happy and well-adjusted. I enjoyed going to his school conferences because his teachers always gave glowing reports of Steve's academic and social accomplishment. In eighth grade, the school counselor told him he had the aptitude, skills, and potential to accomplish anything he set out to do.

A huge change, however, would soon occur in his life. One evening our family gathered around the kitchen table to discuss moving to another state because Ward had decided to enter the ministry. The news was distressing for Steve.

"I don't want to move," he protested, "I don't want to leave my friends." We listened to his plea and then assured him that our family would be together, and we would make the best out of living in a new place. He never said another word about it, but I felt his sadness at leaving the community where he had grown up.

Life on the farm

In spite of his misgivings about uprooting to Ohio, Steve was adaptable. He adjusted well to living in a farm community. His charismatic smile and friendly nature drew new friends immediately, and he soon became involved in school sports and the music program. But he also liked his solitude. He asked for a unicycle for his fourteenth birthday. Back and forth on the dirt driveway from the big farm house to the barn, he would practice balancing on his unicycle.

One day he announced, "I'm going to ride into town," a ten-mile distance from our house.

I asked him, "Do you want one of us to meet you in town to give you a ride back home?"

"No, I can ride both ways," he said matter-of-factly.

When he wasn't home by dinnertime, we got in the car to search for him. Sure enough, we found him peddling his way back home. We stopped the car to ask him if he wanted a lift. He admitted he was tired and reluctantly placed his bike into the trunk of the car. Elated at his accomplishment we all applauded him for his unicycle success.

Steve on his unicycle, age 14, 1975.

Steve was athletic and seemed, at least on the outside, to deal well with defeat. We attended his wrestling matches where once he was pinned in the first minute. Once I found paper cups lying around the house, receptacles into which he constantly spit.

When I asked him why he needed to do this he said, "Mom, I have to remain a certain weight in order to qualify for the light-weight division because they have too many guys in my normal weight category, and the coach recommends this."

I questioned that spitting really helped him maintain his weight.

Although Steve was of slight, 5'8" build, he played high school football. Ward and I went to his games and watched him get tossed around a lot. One evening at the end of the season, he came into our bedroom and said he wanted to talk to us.

"I have to make a difficult decision," he said, "and I need your help."

"What is it," I asked, curious about his struggle. "Well," he said haltingly, "I've been thinking I'll play in the band rather than play football next year."

I was overjoyed at the news. "Dad and I support you in this decision, Steve," I replied.

He seemed to lighten up and be pleased at our conversation as he left our room to go to bed.

To be honest, we were relieved when he decided that his real love was singing in the school chorus, playing his trumpet in the marching band, composing music, and acting in school plays. He lived and breathed music, making the girls swoon when he performed.

He came home one day bubbling with the news that he had been nominated for the King's court. He was one of six boys whose pictures were displayed in the school newspaper for students to vote. Steve was so handsome. I hoped he would be chosen. When the election results were posted, he was disappointed, yet pleased at losing by only a few votes, quite an accomplishment for a student who had only been attending that school for a year. His three years in high school in Ohio were filled with a lot of fun activities and some lonely times for Steve. He seemed to be a loner when he wasn't engaged in school functions. On weekends he stayed home with us and watched TV or made model cars. After Ward's three years in seminary we moved back to Michigan. Once again Steve said goodbye to his friends.

That fall Steve enrolled as a senior in a new high school. Again, it did not take long before he was involved in the music program of his new school. He sang in the chorus and soon spent many hours per week as the music director's right-hand helper at setting up the band room and the stage for their musical productions. At the end of the year, he received an award for his excellent service to the music department. Graduation day was filled with fun where friends and family came to celebrate.

College years

Steve's goal was to play trumpet in the marching band of a Big10 university, so he was excited when he received a music scholarship to Michigan State University. His dormitory was conveniently located near the music buildings, so he could get in his hours of practice and make it back to the dorm where he held a part-time job. His freshman year he excelled in his studies and raved about his music professors. Because the university was only an hour and a half away, we were able to drive there often to attend many of his concerts. I loved watching his face during the chorale presentations. It was obvious he enjoyed singing as he was completely im-

Steve, love that guitar, 1979.

mersed in the harmony of the music he was helping to create. That first year of university life, the only complaint we heard was his girl friend's giving him a hard time. He had found his niche, or so we thought.

However, during his sophomore year he began complaining about some of his classes. I was surprised when he said, "I don't like my music professor. He isn't treating me very well."

We suggested he talk to his adviser and try to work it out. Weeks went by, and we were under the impression that his problems had been resolved.

One day, Steve called saying, "I've decided I want to attend the college in Washington where Kathy went. I don't think I should be here. This university is too big."

"How long have you been feeling that way?" I asked.

"For awhile. I think I should have gone to a smaller college."

Ward and I listened and, somewhat exasperated, agreed that he make arrangements to transfer to the college his sister had attended.

His junior year he packed his bags and traveled to Washington. Soon after he was settled in he called to tell us he was in love with a young woman. I could hear the excitement in his voice.

"Mom," he said, "she is such a sweet person."

With great anticipation, I said, "Dad and I would love to meet her. I'm so happy for you."

However, dissatisfied with the unstructured curriculum at this college, he soon returned to his studies in Michigan without the young woman. The next year his grades dropped. He told us about his gigs playing guitar at the coffee house on campus and how embarrassed he felt when he forgot the words to a song he had sung many times before. We wondered why he was having difficulty when singing was his first love. We were upset but rationalized that he was working late, studying hard, and his forgetfulness was probably due to not getting enough sleep and just coping with the stresses of college life. In hindsight, it is another flag we missed.

That summer Ward was assigned to a church back in our hometown of Grand Rapids, Michigan. Steve came home and helped us move in. He appeared tired. I asked him if he felt okay.

He said, "Oh, I've been smoking marijuana, that's all. Sometimes it makes me sleepy."

I blew up at him. "Steve," I said, in exasperation, "how can you think about smoking pot when you know the problems Carl has experienced with that?"

He brushed me off and didn't want to talk about it further. I have to admit that neither Ward nor I was aware that he might be doing drugs or drinking.

Meanwhile back at college, he began to complain about the difficulty with his studies. Steve had always breezed through his classes, so this development was new for us, especially when he announced he needed to repeat a class because of a low grade. I was getting impatient, convinced

Steve, the charismatic smile, 1983.

he just wasn't applying himself, but I didn't know why. His solution was to change his major. Finally, after five years, he graduated with a degree in humanities. The university placement office set him up with a job interview with a large corporation. Ward and I anticipated he would receive an offer from this company. When he wasn't selected for the job, Steve admitted that when the interviewer asked him what he saw himself doing in five years, Steve had replied, "I want to be a professional musician." We were amused yet baffled that he would be so shortsighted in answering the question that way.

Life after graduation

After graduation we encouraged him to live with us until he could find a full-time job. He settled for part-time work while waiting for the perfect music opportunity to come along.

In the meantime, he entered a lip-synch contest where he imitated Billy Joel playing the harmonica and singing the song, "The Piano Man." He didn't win, but we applauded his acting. Steve seemed to identify with Billy Joel, and he would sit at the piano totally engrossed in playing chords and composing in the style of his idol.

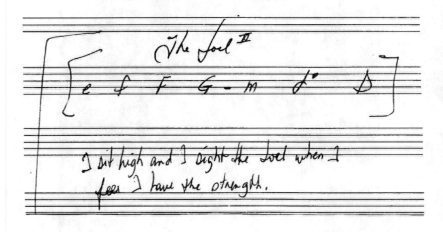

Steve's improvisation of Billy Joel, Grand Rapids, Michigan, 1983.

However, he began to spend more and more time in his room. I could hear the *whrrr* of the electric typewriter behind his closed door. When I asked him to help out around the house, he became angry and resistant.

He said, "I'm busy, Mom. I'm writing a play."

I was happy he was creating, but I was also expecting him to look for work and get on with his life. Ward and I were very frustrated at his opposing everything we said to him. In the spirit of "tough love," we strongly suggested it was time for him to find another place to live since he wasn't cooperating with us. He was surprised that we had suggested he should leave. He mumbled something about moving in with friends then retreated back to his room. Another week went by, and his routine continued. Ward confronted him on what plans he was making, and he admitted he had none. They argued, and Ward told him he needed to leave by the end of the week. Steve said nothing, but angrily went to his room and slammed the door behind him. A few days later he packed up his stuff, informed us that he was moving in with friends, and left. We both felt guilty that he was leaving out of anger, but we agreed it was time for him to be out on his own. I was sure he would eventually find the job he wanted and settle down.

He kept in touch, and after a couple of months he took an apartment on his own.

Signs of a problem

In hindsight, had Ward and I had any clue that Steve might be manifesting mental illness, this whole scenario would have played out differently. As it was, he quit coming to church where he had sung in the choir and was active in the post-graduate group. I thought he was rebelling since he had always obeyed the rules as a youth. He had always been "a good kid."

Wanting to keep the communication open, I called him and left messages but we heard from him less and less. Then the phone woke us from a sound sleep early on New Year's Day.

An officer from the Ohio State Police said, "We have your son, Steve, in custody. Can you come here to pick him up?" He went on to explain, "We apprehended Steve after he drove away from a gas station without paying for the gas."

Aghast and embarrassed, we left at once for Ohio. I had a knot in my stomach when I saw Steve sitting in the police station. He didn't want to look at me, but I gave him a hug, sat down next to him and talked with him about what happened.

"I was on my way to see friends," he said.

It bothered me that he was more philosophical than remorseful, but he assured Ward and me that everything would be fine. Ward made arrangements to pay for the gas, and Steve followed us back home in his car. This was totally out of character for him. I was bewildered at his actions. He paid back the money owed us, but he was becoming more distant every day.

I remember the tension in our relationship on my birthday and how he hardly looked at me as he gave me a framed picture of a bouquet of wispy flowers against a backdrop of midnight blue.

"Thank you, Steve," I said, "this is a beautiful photograph." Feeling his agitation, I asked, "Are you okay?"

"Yup," he replied in a quiet voice.

I felt so helpless when Steve was angry and despondent. When he bottled up his feelings I could only imagine what was happening. I felt as if I was losing him; he wasn't listening to me. I wanted this day to have pleasant memories, so I hung up the picture, purchased with money borrowed from my mother, but the memory of his begrudgingly handing it to me haunted me so that I could hardly enjoy its beauty.

One day, over lunch, I said to him, "Steve, you seem angry with me. Please forgive me if there is something I did that upset you." There was a long silence. "Are you going to tell me what the problem is?" More silence. "Will you forgive me?"

He didn't answer, and I couldn't pull it out of him, so it went unresolved. I felt empty for a long time feeling I had done something to cause him to be so angry and uncommunicative.

A month later we went over to his apartment and noticed boxes stacked up and partially packed. When I commented on this, he said, "I think I'll go to New York and look for a music job."

Ward suggested he wait until he had money saved to pursue that dream, and he seemed to agree with us. One evening, however, unbeknown to us, he loaded his belongings into his truck and disappeared into the night without even a terse goodbye.

Homeless in New York

His landlord called us asking if we knew where Steve had gone. We said no, but we had a hunch he had driven to New York. We debated about going to look for him but had no idea of where to start, so we waited. The first week was hell. After sleepless nights and a week with no word from him, we panicked and called the Missing Person's Bureau. They were blasé about our frantic call and told us they would put Steve's name on a list. However, they said the only possibility of locating him would be by tracing his license plate number if by chance he got picked up for a traffic violation or another offense. They suggested we hire a private detective.

There are no words to describe my feelings of fear, despair and help-lessness. I was in shock that he hadn't called us. I couldn't sleep. I felt so let down by the system. I naively believed that the police somehow would have the networking ability to track down a missing person. As far as I knew, Steve didn't have any credit cards. What would happen if he ran out of money? We racked our brains to figure out a way to reach him. I called a teaching colleague, who had had Steve in his music class, in an attempt to get the phone number of Steve's friend who lived in New York. I bit my lip with hope and anticipation as I dialed the number and talked to his college friend, but in a moment, our hopes were dashed. Steve had neither called him nor stopped by.

I worried about Steve day and night, wondering if he was dead or alive, wondering what he was doing, wondering why he didn't call us. Every time the phone rang or I saw a Dodge Ram truck, my heart would pound in hopes it was Steve.

His birthday came and went without any word from him, and there were the lonely holidays that we traditionally spent together. We con-stantly prayed for his protection and his safe return. People questioned us and made judgments. "You'd think he would have called by now." The apprehension of not knowing where he was and the strain of seeing his younger brother, Carl, struggle daily with mental illness, was spilling over into Ward's work and mine.

We sought the professional help of a psychologist. We saw her indi-vidually, then met together for the last two sessions. After three months of therapy, we both were able to release some of the old, "stuck" patterns, beliefs, and attitudes that had shaped us as children. I examined my fear and anger at Steve's disappearing and explored new ways to express my fear. The more I talked about my pain, the more I could forgive Steve and myself, and I found some solace and relief.

Ward, in turn, focused on working through his fear of Steve's not returning. Although the counselor was kind and compassionate in presenting the possibility of Steve's death, Ward found this an agonizing idea that neither his heart nor his mind could accept.

Steve is alive

We agonized for a long, lonely year and a half waiting for some word from Steve. Finally, one hot summer's day in July, Steve called, and our long wait was over. When Ward answered the phone and heard Steve's voice, it took his breath away. Steve was sobbing and laughing at the same time, overcome with emotion, as he talked to his dad for the first time in so many months. The joy and relief Ward felt at hearing Steve's voice was soon mixed with fear and apprehension when he learned that Steve was phoning from the psychiatric ward of New York's Bellevue Hospital. Ward called me at my mom's house immediately.

I yelled into the phone, "He really called? Is he okay? Tell me his exact words." I was ecstatic to know Steve was alive. I couldn't get home fast enough to return Steve's call and hear his voice.

As I listened to the familiar yet alien voice at the other end of the phone, I was shocked and dismayed to hear his recounting of his recent experiences.

"I've been here for two weeks," he stammered. I was also taken aback to hear him slurring words as he spoke. "The staff told me to call you when I was ready. I lived on the streets of New York for eighteen months." I wanted to scream into the phone, "You did what? Why? Why were you homeless when we were here for you all along?" But I let him speak, uninterrupted. I thirsted for every detail of every minute he had spent apart from us, as painful as it was to hear his words.

He continued, "I stayed in public buildings at night when I wasn't found out, wasn't kicked out. People gave me money for food."

I couldn't believe what I was hearing, but it wasn't even the full story. He was evasive when I asked him what had happened to his truck and belongings. His healthcare workers later filled in some gaps.

New York Mayor Ed Koch's "Team of Hope" workers had observed Steve loitering in the streets of Greenwich Village for one month. They explained: "We picked him up after he fainted while standing in a food line. He was suffering not only from malnutrition and a celiac disease, but he also couldn't even carry on an intelligible conversation."

Diagnosis

"So what is his prognosis?" I asked, hoping it would be good news.

They continued, "Upon admittance to Bellevue hospital, he was diagnosed with undifferentiated schizophrenia."

This can't be true, I thought. There must be some mistake. Ward and I couldn't comprehend that we might have two sons with mental illness. Ward talked with Steve's psychiatrist about his condition and made arrangements to have him discharged into our daughter's care as she lived nearby. Marcia took charge of him but was shocked to see her handsome brother now disheveled, emaciated, gaunt, sunken eyed and with a very short haircut. We learned later that he threw his medication away shortly after arriving at Marcia's house, and we never realized he was given a prescription for an anti-psychotic drug, Haldol, upon his discharge. Having lived and dealt with his brother's symptoms, I suspect Steve was too scared to face the fact that he might suffer from the same problems, so he refused to take the medication he had received in the hospital.

We sent him money for a plane ticket home and sat back, trying to prepare for his arrival. I was anxious about both his mental and physical condition, and, at the same time, desperate to know about the details of his life in New York. When he arrived, I couldn't believe my eyes. I was shocked at his appearance. He was so thin; he looked like a prisoner of war. We each gave him a big hug, told him how much we loved him and tried to let him settle in. I didn't want to press him, but I had so many questions. What had happened to his truck and his belongings? Where did he stay? Did he ever seek employment? How did he survive eighteen months in cold New York City, "the Big Apple," the place of his dreams, without any income?

I never heard the whole story. He either didn't remember everything or was too embarrassed to share it with us. He filled in some of the details.

"I think the police impounded my truck," he said sheepishly. "I don't know if we can get it back now." He seemed to want to talk so we sat and listened. "I managed to get money from strangers once in a while and a blanket or another layer of clothes from other street people when I was cold. Except for a fight in the Bowery, people were good to me."

"What happened in the Bowery?" we asked. "There was an abandoned building about the size of a warehouse where people stayed at night. One guy came along and stole my bread. I ran after him, and he stabbed me."

I had a lump in my throat as I listened to his horrific experiences. I wasn't sure I wanted to hear anymore.

"Look," he said, as he pulled his shirt off. "I have several stab wounds on my back and side."

Ward and I looked at the scars on his body. "Oh, Steve," I said holding back the tears, "I'm so sorry you had these horrible experiences." I had wanted to ask him about the scars on his leg and decided this was a good time. "Steve, what happened to your legs?"

He hesitated, but slowly rolled up his pant leg to expose hundreds of bruises all over both legs. They were all about the size of a dime, and they were brown and gross.

"The nurse told me this is from malnutrition," he said sadly. "Hopefully they will fade."

"Yes," I said, trying to sound reassuring, "I'm sure they will as you begin to heal emotionally and physically."

Steve moved in with Carl, who was glad to have his brother back in town because they could get back to their music again. They spent hours improvising and composing catchy tunes. Carl wrote clever lyrics while Steve made up the jazzy tunes on his guitar. Steve soon held a part-time job as a cashier at a movie theatre.

Homeless in California

Three months later, Carl called us. "Mom, I think Steve left town this afternoon. I think he went to California."

"What makes you believe that?" I asked.

"His clothes are gone, and my one hundred dollar bill is missing from my bank. I think he took it," Carl said sadly.

I felt so angry and helpless at not being able to avert what I perceived to be another downward spiral.

We didn't call the Missing Person's Bureau, but we worried and waited. It doesn't matter what age your child is, you always have a heart connection to them. Until you know they are safe, there is no rest. We had no other recourse but to pray for him. We set a plate at the dinner table for him at Thanksgiving and Christmas, praying he would show up.

"We will hear from him," I said, hopefully.

This time three months passed before Ward and I knew where Steve was. We learned of his whereabouts when we received a summons forwarded to our address from the Santa Monica police department. Steve had gotten a ticket for jaywalking. We were relieved to know he was alive.

On my birthday, in January, the phone rang. "Hi, Mom, Happy Birthday," said Steve.

"It's you!" I exclaimed. I was thrilled to hear from him. "Where are you?"

"I'm calling from a pay phone in Santa Monica."

"Give me the phone number, and we'll call you tomorrow at the same time," I said excitedly. I quickly wrote down the number. After chatting awhile, he agreed to meet us the first Saturday in March on the Santa Monica pier.

The next day I tried to reach him at the number he had given us. As I pictured a phone booth somewhere in Santa Monica, the phone rang and rang. To my surprise, after seven or eight rings, someone answered, and I had a short conversation with this stranger. I asked if Steve was around. He called out to a couple of people asking them if they knew Steve, but to no avail. I asked him where this phone booth was located, and he told me it was in a strip mall in Santa Monica.

We flew to California to see Steve. When he called me on my birthday he assured us he had written down the date and the place we would meet. That day arrived, and Ward and I greeted the dawn with elation. We were anticipating seeing Steve after his six-months' absence, but my hopes were dashed when he didn't show up as agreed. I had lost him again.

An angel

Back home, I fell back into my old, now familiar pattern of thought. *Where is he? What is he doing?* After two agonizingly long months, I picked up the telephone to hear the voice of a woman whom I would come to call "Steve's angel."

She introduced herself as Juanita and said, "I saw Steve walking along the street, and I invited him out for lunch. I want you to know he is okay." I was so joyful to hear this good news. Juanita continued, "I was only with him a short time, but I know Steve is very special. I told him to call home."

I said, "How did you know our phone number?"

She replied, "I asked Steve about his family and where you lived. Then immediately after leaving him, I went to the library to look up your number."

I believe it was Juanita's spirit of unconditional love that prompted Steve to call the next day. "Hi, Mom," he said. Those two simple words, "Hi, Mom," stirred such a deep love in my heart. "I'm thinking about coming home, but I'm waiting for a big deal to come through with Fox studios."

I had a sinking feeling that this young man was in trouble, at best; delusional at worst, and needed to come home immediately.

"I'll call you tomorrow," he said. He hung up so abruptly that I felt fearful that it would be months before we heard from him again, but he called us back the following day as promised. He said, "I lost my wallet and ID, so I can't buy an airline ticket."

"We'll make arrangements to wire you money for a bus ticket home," I said.

Time stopped as we stood and waited for the bus to arrive. I was so happy I would finally be reunited with Steve. I had missed him so much. The bus stopped and I watched expectantly as each person descended the stairs and walked away. Some were greeted by loved ones and others were alone. The bus emptied and Steve wasn't there.

"Oh, my God," I said to Ward, "what's wrong now? Where is he?"

I couldn't believe he wasn't on the bus. I didn't know whether to scream or cry! We asked the driver if he had seen him, and he gave us a curt, "No." We checked the schedule only to find that the next bus wouldn't arrive until the following morning. I was going crazy! I didn't know if I could wait another day. Disappointed and frustrated, we left knowing we would be there in the morning. The next day I prayed, "Please God, let Steve be on this bus." Again, we waited and watched each person as they exited the bus.

"There he is," I said to Ward excitedly. I was so relieved when I saw him coming toward us. Here was my dear son, scruffy, unkempt, unshaven, clothed in dirty garments. Despite his appearance, he was a sight for sore eyes. I didn't care what he looked like, I was just so happy to see him again. Steve looked embarrassed—I know he didn't want us to see him looking this way—but he gave us each a hug anyway and let us take him home. I asked him why he hadn't been on the bus the evening before. He casually told us that when he had gone for something to eat he missed the bus, so he slept in the station and caught the first available bus home. I felt like strangling this kid!

Home again

The first thing he did was to take a shower. After that and a much-needed haircut, he was magically transformed into the handsome young man I remembered, at least on the outside.

He abruptly said, "I'm going over to live with Carl."

"Oh, Steve," I said, "Carl is living in a group home, so you'll need to stay with us. Do you want the upstairs bedroom? Or you can make yourself a place in the basement." He thought for a moment, then chose the basement.

The next week, we drove to our cottage to celebrate his twenty-seventh birthday. He said he wanted a skateboard. I blew this request off as an adolescent desire and instead gave him some much-needed clothes for his birthday. I was angry, tired, frustrated and scared, and I wasn't into shopping for a skateboard. However, I noticed the disappointed look on his face as he opened his brightly wrapped birthday package only to find a new pair of jeans and a shirt.

He found employment once more, and I was hopeful things would return to normal. However, after work one evening, I observed him talking to himself.

I asked him, "What's going on, Steve?"

"I'm just thinking out loud about what happened to me in New York and California," he replied snappily.

This was the end of the discussion as far as he was concerned, but I now knew he needed professional help. My worst fear was that he, like his brother, needed medication for what was becoming obvious yet so painful for me to admit. He was manifesting symptoms of mental illness similar to those that Carl had been treated for the past eight years. I knew that without medication his symptoms were exacerbating.

He finally admitted he couldn't cope or concentrate very well and agreed to see a psychologist.

"How did your appointment work out with the psychologist?" I asked, when he returned home.

"Okay," he replied. "I filled out some forms, and she wants me to come back, but I'm not sure if I will."

Steve, the lost returns, 1988.

He lost his job after working only two weeks and became increasingly agitated and withdrawn.

"How about getting treatment at the hospital, Steve?" I asked.

"Absolutely not," I heard him saying quietly, his voice trailing off. I recall thinking I should admit him on an involuntary basis, but I hesitated to provoke a scene. Hindsight, however, tells me the hospital might not have admitted him since the criteria for admittance is that a person must be a danger to himself or to others, and we saw no signs of that behavior.

Knowing how much he loved to perform, I asked him to sing a duet with me at church. Since he was being very uncommunicative, I put a note on his bathroom mirror to remind him of our Sunday morning engagement. Fortunately, we had both sung these songs before so we didn't need much rehearsal. Although he was agitated, he showed up at church and eloquently played a guitar accompaniment. I loved harmonizing with him. It was like melding our two hearts together in love. During this joyful moment, I had no idea that this was the last song we would ever sing together.

The next day began in an uneventful manner. Ward and I went out separately and ran errands. Ward returned home first and, to his eternal dismay, found Steve hanging from the rafters in the basement of the parsonage. I arrived fifteen minutes later, having turned in my grades at the university, happy and excited to be off for the summer.

As I turned the corner onto our street, I saw lights flashing on the E-unit in front of our house. I pulled into the driveway and hurriedly jumped out of my car, not even bothering to close the door. My heart filled with dread. From the anguish on Ward's face, I knew something was horribly wrong.

He ran to me crying, "Steve's dead! Steve's dead!" His words were incomprehensible.

"What happened?" I stammered in disbelief.

"I found him hanging above my workbench. I hugged him hoping he was still breathing but he was so cold. He is still there, Mary. Don't go down there," Ward pleaded.

"Oh, no, no, no!" I sobbed. "Not our beloved son! No, no, no, no!" The pain was agonizing, insufferable. We held each other and wept. And wept. And wept.

The Soul

They touched my soul with their cold hearts, but I will lead them through the night with no fear in sight.

The passage to the opening of their minds was occupied by the deep breath of mankind.

We did not take for granted the presence of God's way though the way was preoccupied by tests of courage and bravery.

Were as it was, was as it is, the people's court crucified all there was — but it came about to be all right.

All right to be called a man, all right to be called a woman.

Carl J. Scovel
Age 26
September 1990

Carl, Suzuki violin lessons, 1968.

4

Carl's Incredible Courage

"They touched my soul with their cold hearts,
but I will lead them through the night with no fear in sight."

Carl J. Scovel

Our second son

Carl had incredible strength of character and a strong love for his family. He always had a good word for everyone he met and would give you the shirt off his back. Even during adversity, he kept his wonderful sense of humor.

We were delighted with the birth of our first son but equally joyful with the arrival of our second. The boys would be buddies.

A visit to the pediatrician revealed news that Carl's legs were turned outward and a brace attached to the bottom of his shoes would keep his legs straight and in line. It seemed so cruel to restrict a baby that way. I thought this would slow him down, but Carl was not to be deterred by a mere brace. He scooted around the floor and kept up with his brother and sisters. After six months the brace came off, and he began pulling himself up on the furniture. We knew we had an athlete in our family. He was our energizer bunny as he went from cupboard to cupboard to investigate all the shiny pots and pans, and everything in his path.

As well as being the first of our children to climb out of his crib, Carl was also the first and only one of our children to attend a preschool twice a week for the year before entering kindergarten. Because his brother and sisters were in school, we enrolled him in hopes of giving him an opportunity to socialize with other children his age. His teachers reported that he was content but shy, and stayed to himself much of the time.

In grade school, some of his favorite songs were about Davy Crockett and Daniel Boone. Not a day would go by without his wearing Daniel Boone boots made from a soft doeskin. I loved to watch him gently slide on each boot and ritualistically pull the laces until it fit his foot tightly, then slip his squirrel tailed hat on and run off to play. He was so fond of that particular pair of boots that when he outgrew them, he knew the exact shelf and which store to look for the same, special pair.

Life in Ohio

Carl was twelve years old when we moved to Ohio. He made some good friends.

Soon after school started in the fall, I received a call from the principal. "Carl has been brought to my office for getting in a fight," his stern voice reported.

I immediately went to the school; and, as events unfolded, I learned that Carl had been reprimanded by the principal and the punishment was paddling.

"You paddled my son?" I said angrily.

"This is our discipline policy," he said, backing away and getting defensive. I was outraged and told him I disapproved of this kind of discipline. Then I asked Carl, "How did the fight begin?"

He said, "Someone was teasing me for being in class with the dummies."

What do you mean, 'dummies'?"

"I'm not in classes with the friends I hang around with," he said, almost crying at this point.

"Why not? Can you explain this to me?" I said, turning to the counselor.

The counselor showed me Carl's academic records from his previous school. I looked over the rows of columns with average scores. In order to understand what was happening, I went to school the next day to observe his classroom. When I walked in and looked around, I understood what Carl was telling me. The children seemed to be lethargic and disinterested in their environment. Having been trained in special education, I suspected these children needed more help than Carl. At that moment, my thoughts were interrupted by the teacher's calling on Carl to read. The teacher complimented him for being so articulate and reading so well. I was puzzled and angry as to why he was in this class. Afterwards, his teacher was very compassionate and admitted she wasn't sure why Carl had been placed with her schoolroom of slow learners either, so I hastened to the principal's office. I demanded Carl be placed in a curriculum of his academic level which would put him back with his friends. They agreed and apologized for the mistake of reading the records incorrectly and making a hasty placement. Carl was much happier being with his friends again, and the fighting stopped.

That year, at age thirteen, he went out for Little League baseball. He was so proud of his baseball mitt and was so handsome in his red and white striped outfit. He especially liked playing second base. He caught the line drives with ease and made force plays to get the opponents out when they were coming into second. When his team won a game, he loved going out to the favorite local pizza place with the coach, his team members, and some of the parents.

On to high school

In high school, Carl had caught up to Steve in height and eventually surpassed his big brother's weight by about five pounds. Being in prime physical condition and slightly more aggressive than Steve, he was anxious to play guard on the school football team. When he came out of the huddle, he had the determined look of Dick Butkus to go out on the field and give it his all.

In ninth grade, after the school ran a screening program for signs of scoliosis, we received disappointing news that Carl had a curvature in his spine. The report indicated that it wasn't a major curve, but suggested he come in for periodic checkups. The following year we took him to a chiropractor who treated his condition with a girdle brace that fit around his torso. Although he complained about wearing it, he admitted it supported him. He demonstrated courage while wearing it for eighteen months, which alleviated the need for surgery.

I would describe Carl as very spiritual, easily grasping the meaning of life. He had a lot of common sense, yet many unfulfilled aspirations. He could sing, play the violin, and write poetry and was a sensitive artist who could draw and paint. He loved girls and had an effervescent sense of humor.

Carl was a typical teenager. Like most kids, he experimented and tested limits that I considered normal. I felt the common challenges of mothering an adolescent and worried, as mothers do, about drugs, sex, and his relationships with other kids.

Soon after Carl had his driver's license, he asked permission to take my car to pick up his friend. Later that evening when Ward and I drove into the garage, I was shocked to see the Dodge Colt.

I said to Ward, "Do you see what I see?" There wasn't an inch of metal that wasn't dented. Upset, we hurried into the house and found Carl sitting there sheepishly waiting for us to return home.

He explained, "I kinda lost control of the car, and my friend and I turned over in a ditch. I immediately started the car and drove out of the ditch. I dropped my friend off at his house and drove home. I'm really sorry."

Luckily no one was hurt, and we had insurance on the car. One of the consequences of his accident was losing a good friend whose mother wouldn't let him hang around with Carl anymore.

Carl was not a bad boy, but he had been arrested in the eleventh grade. The voice of the police officer jarred me as I answered the phone. Carl and his friend had been picked up a block from our house because they were in violation for smoking marijuana.

Carl told us this story. "We stopped to have one joint, and when we saw the police I threw the joint under the car. They found it and took us to the police station."

I was upset that he was smoking, but his sister chided him saying, "Carl, at least you could have rubbed it out with your shoe."

We had suspected Carl was smoking because his eyes looked red and sore some of the time. Unfortunately, in spite of our talks with him about the dangers of smoking, he continued to smoke with his friends off school grounds and away from our house so we wouldn't know.

Ward and I went to court with Carl. Since he was a minor and had never been in trouble before, he was put on probation for six months. To my great relief, he wouldn't have a record due to the First Offender Act. Because we had just moved from the country back to the city, I was convinced his behavior would change as soon as he made new friends and felt at home in this new school and church group.

Carl adapted to the city by joining the cross-country team and the school chorus. He and his brother were especially good buddies. They made a good team, because while Steve was rather naïve but quick witted, Carl had common sense and an acute awareness of his environment. One evening Steve asked Carl to ride with him while he delivered pizza. As they were approaching a rough part of town, Steve slowed down the car to make a phone call to get directions.

As he began pulling into a gas station, Carl said, "Don't stop here, Steve. There's a group of guys over there, and I don't have a good feeling about this."

Steve, the big brother, ignored Carl's plea. A few seconds after Steve stepped out of the car, two guys came toward him and began beating on him, then took all his money.

Meanwhile, a huge man, as described by Carl, walked over to Carl's side of the car, showed him his gun and ordered him to open the window. Trembling, Carl obediently rolled down the window as the man flashed a knife and demanded, in a loud voice, "Give me your class ring or I'll cut your finger off." Carl hurriedly took off his brand new gold class ring and gave it to the man.

At this point, Steve ran to the car, started the motor and sped away, finally safe, but very scared and humiliated from their horrendous experience. Steve never lived it down and more than once, Carl teased his brother saying, "I told you so."

Though he had a great relationship with his brother, at school he fell in with friends whose influence I considered detrimental to his greater good. That school year, Carl not only was arrested and totaled my car, but he also had bouts with depression. I was convinced it was all drug-related.

The summer before Carl began his senior year in high school, Ward was assigned to a church as senior pastor, so we moved again to a new community. Our daughter, Marcia, was in the Peace Corps in Sierra Leone, Africa, while her sister, Kathy, was attending a college in Washington State. We were pleased this move would take Carl away from bad influences.

New town, new school

In order to get acquainted in a new town, Steve and Carl marketed themselves as "Music Messengers." Carl was the lyricist and Steve the composer. They wrote songs for special occasions and would take their violin and trumpet to a person's home to entertain them with a specially written song or ditty. The boys were featured in a newspaper article with their picture. They also made a cassette tape of "Fanagel the Bagel," a funny song Carl composed and sang with Steve backing him on the guitar. Carl even went around to local bagel stores and tried to sell them on the idea of using the song for their logo.

On the first day of his senior year at a new school, the kids, wanting to get acquainted, rallied around Carl. I was encouraged with his adjustment at this new school when he proudly announced that he had joined the cross-country track team, was playing violin in the orchestra, and was chosen by the choir director to be in a male quartet. I was very happy that he seemed to be making friends and liked school.

About three months into the fall semester, Carl began to show signs of stress, anxiety and depression. I thought some of his pain might be that he missed his brother who had left that fall for college.

In light of growing signs of stress, I decided to talk with his counselor at school, only to find out that he wasn't completing assignments and was skipping classes. I began to wonder if his change in behavior was more than drug-related. To my astonishment, his counselor knew nothing about symptoms of mental illness nor did she seem to care. She only wanted me to know his orchestra teacher suspected that he might be tak-

Carl, cross country, 1981.

ing drugs. When we confronted him about drug use, he vehemently denied any involvement. I worried as I saw him changing, losing interest in school.

Things went from bad to worse when his art teacher called. Her voice was stern. "Carl made a sculpture of a person representing the high school and put an arrow through its heart. I am very upset, and his friends are confused."

Because of his change in behavior, his friends no longer wanted to be around him and, in fact, would make fun of him. It hurt me to see them roll their eyes and laugh after Carl spoke and eventually they left him out of their activities. Carl then had few options as to what friends he hung around with. The boys who came to our house appeared to lack the values and morals that Carl held. We came home one evening to find a gouge in our antique dining room table. The next morning, as Ward went to reach for his razor, much to his dismay found it missing. I was upset that these new "friends" were taking advantage of Carl. It was a dilemma. He wanted to be accepted by his peers. I longed for him to have a good buddy.

Then one day I came home and found him sitting on the floor playing his guitar.

"Look, Mom, I'm Jesus Christ."

I gazed into his eyes when I heard his tone of voice, a knot in my stomach telling me that he wasn't kidding. He was convinced, at that moment, that he was indeed Jesus the Christ.

In light of these negative behavior patterns, I made an appointment for Carl to see a psychologist who recommended ongoing therapy. During that year of weekly talk therapy, however, his behavior remained basically unchanged.

Symbolic of his progressive turning inward, Carl moved his bed to the basement. When I questioned why he wanted to be down there, he was irritated and said, "It's dark there, and I can sleep better."

The same day, I saw him toss his pottery artwork into the lake behind the house. When I asked him why, he nonchalantly replied, "It's my old stuff. I don't need it anymore."

"But Carl," I pleaded, "those were your beautifully designed ceramic pieces."

"It's a bunch of junk," he said dejectedly.

At that moment, I realized the seriousness of this behavior.

The diagnosis

I knew the symptoms of mental illness all too well through my work in a psychiatric hospital as a music therapist. I was still pretty much in denial about the possibility, but the thought still entered my mind, *Could Carl be mentally ill?*

The psychologist also suggested that Carl might require a psychiatrist as he seemed to need more than talk therapy. The psychiatrist diagnosed him as having schizophrenia.

"He has what? I don't believe it. How do you know this?" I questioned.

I was told that the results of the battery of tests given to Carl indicated schizophrenia. I was so sad and frustrated at this news and, at the same time, determined to find a way to help my son overcome this illness. He was only seventeen years old.

Taking Carl to his doctor and group therapy appointments as well as monitoring his medications began my involvement in the world of mental illness as a parent rather than as a professional. Over the next thirteen years, Ward, Carl and I—and to some extent the rest of the family—met challenges on a daily basis. During this time, Carl spent some time living with us, followed by entry into the mental health system which involved staying in

Carl, his many faces, 1982.

independent living accommodations and eventually in a group home. Interspersed were many periods of hospitalization.

Following his diagnosis, Carl lived at home for about eight years. His initial response to coping with his illness was to quit high school in April. I was frantic! I called our family friend, Millie, and talked with her about Carl's actions. Two days later he received a letter from her encouraging him to return to school.

"You need those papers, Carl," she wrote. Carl loved Millie, and he took her words seriously. I'm sure that Millie was Carl's guardian angel because finally, after much struggle and talking to him about the importance of a high school diploma, he reluctantly returned to school in May to make up his work and graduate with his class.

That fall he enrolled at a junior college and completed his first semester, but his illness manifested as auditory hallucinations and paranoia. One day he walked into his government class and announced that the police were following him. Everyone laughed at him, of course, for he looked strange adorned in his long trench coat and straw hat. When his professor called me at work about his strange behavior, I left immediately and picked him up at school. That ended his college career.

For the next few years, as Carl struggled to cope with his illness, he wrote poetry, painted many Picasso-style pictures, played his violin, and attempted to find part-time work. He continued to live at home and received outpatient care. His medications kept his condition stable.

In the meantime his sister, Kathy, and her future husband came to stay. The three of them found employment at the same place, and Carl felt a lot of support from them. However, this didn't eliminate the symptoms that caused some bizarre behavior.

One night I found him outside at 1:00 a.m. playing his violin, and he had no understanding of the problem this presented for the neighbors. On another occasion, I received a call from a family in a town sixty miles away telling me that they had picked up Carl hitchhiking along the highway and that they were concerned about him. Ward and I went immediately to pick him up, and again he had no conception of the repercussions of his act.

Carl often took walks, and one particular evening he heard noises behind him. He threw his new coat and new Walkman down on the ground and ran because he was afraid that the three boys following him were going to hurt him. Carl was 6'1" and though the likelihood of attack was slight, his paranoia was heightened. The next day Ward and I went to retrieve his belongings, but they were gone.

When his sister decided to relocate, Carl lost part of the fabric of his support system and additional medication couldn't alleviate symptoms.

First hospitalization

His psychiatrist recommended that he be hospitalized, and a few weeks later he was admitted for the first time to a private psychiatric hospital due to a psychotic break. He was nervous but I assured him that receiving treatment was the right decision. We had to wait in the lobby for several hours. When his name was finally called, the administrative assistant berated him for "having an attitude." I saw a scared young man with his head down, giving the hospital personnel no eye contact let alone any signs of an attitude. They took him away to the unit, telling Ward and me we could see him the next day. But the next day came and went. When we were finally allowed to see Carl later that week, he was zombie-like and lethargic, the result of too much medication. I questioned the doctor about Carl's state of mind and dosage. The next time we visited Carl, he was much clearer, and we were able to have a nice conversation with him. At that time Carl told us that, in the past year or so, he and his friends had taken every street drug including a hit of LSD. I was furious hearing this news, and for the first time we began to wonder if his illness was drug-induced.

One week after his admission to the hospital we received a call from the police telling us that Carl had escaped from the psychiatric unit by bending a spoon to open the window. My first reaction was anger at the hospital personnel for this breach of security.

"Where do you think he is?" I said to Ward. "Do you think he'd walk or hitchhike to our cottage since he knows we're here for the weekend? I'm so worried he'll wander around and be hungry and in danger. I don't think he has any money."

We waited in a state of deep emotional anguish until the hospital personnel called us two days later. The police had picked him up about ten miles away. They saw him walking along the road near the next town and returned him to the hospital. We were relieved to know he was safe.

When he was discharged, I was sure he would emerge cured from this treatment. Much to my consternation, however, I found that the cycle repeated itself again and again; he would be hospitalized many, many, more times.

It became apparent during the eight years Carl lived with us that his brain disease was cyclical. Every year, in May or June, he would have a setback and become too stressed to work. Carl was employed as a custodian for a company whose policy was to hire people on disability. After holding a job for eighteen months and getting satisfactory reviews, he was fired for having too many sick days. When he told me he was fired, I was upset. As far as we knew, he was doing more than a satisfactory job for the company since only a month before he had been chosen to appear in the company's promotion video. I didn't understand why they would fire him knowing about his illness.

"Did they ask you why you missed those days of work," I asked?

"No one would believe me anyway," he said. We spoke to the mental health worker in charge there, but he wasn't able to change their decision. This cycle left him discouraged, and each time led to a downward spiral of despair. In response, he was often given different or more medication, as his doctors continued to try and find the correct dosage for his schizophrenia prescription.

In an attempt to increase his independence and self-confidence, he moved into a duplex which we purchased. In this setting he received a combination of professional and family support which gave Carl an opportunity to gain independent living skills. As the symptoms progressed, he once again found himself on an escalating path of medication with indescribable side effects. When Carl would choose to go off his medications because of the horrible side effects of constipation, dry mouth, and tremors, he would then become psychotic leading again to periods of hospitalization.

Alternative treatment program

Knowing the limitation that drugs placed on his ability to function normally, I was always searching for ways to improve Carl's quality of life. A friend told me about an alternative treatment program in California at which the director of the program claimed to have had success in getting people with schizophrenia off their toxic medication. The program also included good nutrition, exercise, personal and work responsibility, and socialization. Ward talked with the director who himself had recovered from schizophrenia and was now dedicated to helping others. We questioned him as to his recovery, and he gave us impressive statistics: one third of the people diagnosed with schizophrenia recover and live a normal life without taking medication. I also spoke with parents whose children he had helped, and they spoke highly of him and of the treatment center. I investigated the program thoroughly, and Carl decided he'd like to go there for treatment. Carl's case manager warned us about moving Carl to a new program but assured us that he could re-enter their program if he needed their services in the future. I was confident he wouldn't need them again. This would be the program that would heal him.

Three months later we planned a trip to California to see both boys. First we visited Carl at the treatment center. I was encouraged to see him acting happier and looking better than he had in a long time. His home and accommodations were quite comfortable. We took Carl and the director out for lunch.

Carl said, "Order the mahi-mahi fish, Mom and Dad. It's delicious."

It was the first time either Ward or I had had this delicious pink fish, so popular in Hawaii.

The next day, with the director's permission, we picked up Carl. We drove to the Santa Monica pier to meet Steve, but he didn't show up. It had been five months since Steve had mysteriously disappeared for the second time. I had had a phone call from him promising to meet us at the pier on this day in March. Needless to say, Ward, Carl, and I were terribly disappointed. After walking the beach with Carl and having a bite to eat, we took him back to the treatment center. I hugged him and said goodbye, assured that he would be home soon since he was showing signs of fine progress.

We flew home the next day only to find a shocking message on our answering machine. "Call the treatment center; Carl is in jail." Upset and disconcerted by the tone of the message, Ward and I called immediately.

The director offered this story. "Carl was working in the furniture store that I own. He went outside and began talking to some people. I asked him to return to the store. Carl refused and became very agitated and began yelling at me. I called the police, and they handcuffed him and took him away."

"Why did you do that?" I asked.

"He was very disruptive," he continued. "It was your visit that was the catalyst for his psychotic reaction."

I shouted, "We entrusted our son to your care, but when Carl went out of control, you called the police and then blamed us for Carl's actions." Ward and I were fuming.

Ward talked to the police at the jail, who relayed to us that since Carl was calm and settled down, he would be transferred to a psychiatric ward the next day. I talked with Carl then, to get his version of what had occurred.

He told me his side of the story. "The director was upset because he didn't want anyone in the community to know he was housing four patients. It seems that his center, which is his home, isn't zoned for commercial business."

I was inclined to believe Carl because he was usually straight with us; however, the truth was probably somewhere in between both stories. I held such hope that this was the perfect opportunity for Carl to become well, and he, too, seemed excited about the prospect of being free of medication. Ward and I were angry at the way the director handled the situation. We told him, not only of our disappointment with his actions, but that we wouldn't recommend his program.

I was amazed that Carl kept a good attitude, a loving spirit, and a great sense of humor in the face of this adversity. "The food in jail is good," he said. I've met this great 'dude' who plays the guitar, so we're rocking and rolling together here."

Part of Ward's and my reason for calling was to discuss his options, after which he decided to return to Michigan. I made arrangements for his release, and he flew home immediately.

Independent living

Upon his return from California, we contacted his case manager who placed him in an apartment house with a roommate. Although a stranger, Carl worked at getting along and making a friend of his new roommate. Likewise, he worked at finding satisfying employment. But as time passed, the cycle of crisis that would terminate his work continued. In spite of this setback, Carl continued on the medication regime and continued to suffer the ill effects of these powerful and toxic drugs. After being gone for eight months, Steve returned in May, close to his twenty-seventh birthday, and Carl was delighted to have his brother back. During this time, they shared their love of music that resulted in more new compositions and enjoyed spending time on the lake taking turns water skiing and driving the speedboat.

When Carl received the news of his beloved brother's unexpected death, he sought solace from the family that had always been there for him in his time of need. But in his suffering, he found the depth of courage to offer support as well. A tragic moment brought to life the true essence of Carl's heart and soul. No one would have blamed him if he couldn't have dealt with the loss of his brother and best friend given the incredible circumstances of his own life. And yet he bravely faced his grief, anger, and sorrow in communion with those he loved.

I can only guess that one of the many ways he dealt with his feeling of loss was by starting the habit of smoking which he had always disdained. However, I don't have to guess the ways he helped me deal with my loss, because his love was such a source of strength as he ministered to his dad, his sisters, and me.

After Steve's death, Carl returned to his life of menial work, idle time, loneliness, frustration, and coping with the ongoing side effects of his medications. Carl considered his jobs to be menial in comparison to those held by family members who were college graduates. Although I encouraged him to take pride in whatever he undertook, his own standards for success left him feeling unfulfilled and frustrated in the types of jobs he could get.

Whether his illness, his brother's death, or some other circumstances provided the prompt, Carl felt the need to purchase a .22 caliber rifle and ammunition which he kept out of sight in his closet. To our knowledge, the gun was never fired; and, when Ward was notified by his roommate of its existence, he quickly went to Carl's apartment and removed it. When asked about the gun, Carl had little to say about the whole incident.

Group home

This series of events led Carl's case manager to reevaluate his needs, and the decision was made for him to enter a group home where he would live in a more structured environment with more regular contact by mental health professionals.

I remember the day Carl moved into the home. The director immediately introduced us to the young man with whom he would share the second floor and to the other two men who lived downstairs.

We walked up the stairs to a dimly lit room on the second floor of the house.

"This is your bedroom, and here is the key to lock the door," the director said to Carl. I walked around the apartment in horror at what I saw. The walls in the living room needed painting and there were cigarette burns on the wooden arms of the chairs. The bathroom was small, and there was a gaping hole under the shower. *How can I possibly leave my son here?* I thought. I had a knot in my stomach. I looked over at Carl who appeared unaffected by his new environment. He and his dad were happily hanging up the light blue, silky curtains Carl had picked out in preparation for the move. Knowing how Carl loved beauty in his life, I made a gorgeous multi-colored quilt for him. I loved piecing the shapes and designs together, and with every stitch I said a prayer for him. His quilt held a touch of my love. It was time to see how it fit into the color scheme of the room. Excited, I laid the newly made quilt on his bed. Carl looked at it and then at me, smiled a huge smile, and gave me a hug.

"That is a beautiful quilt, Mom. Thank you."

My heart was overjoyed. I kissed him goodbye and left him to settle in.

A few days later Carl called us. "When are you coming to visit? I have a surprise for you."

The following weekend we were delighted to see his bedroom walls covered with his poems and artwork. His room now reflected his essence. Each week we took him out to dinner and shared the events of the past week. Often I dreaded this reunion because I never knew what mood he would be in. Sometimes he would slouch down in his seat at the restaurant and speak in a very low voice, not wanting to talk, while at other times, we would enjoy laughing together.

I was grateful to his case managers who checked up on him in his group home. On one random call, they found Carl in his room, lying in a pool of blood with his wrists slashed. They called 911 and had him admitted to the hospital. Another time they found him on his bed almost unconscious from an overdose of medication and took him to the hospital to have his stomach pumped. After these suicide attempts, he was placed in a crisis home until he became stabilized, then sent back to his group home and his job.

Bid for fame

In spite of all the problems he endured, Carl was unique. He was creative, loving and persevering. His goal was to be famous. In his junior year in high school, he displayed his artwork in the local library and even sold one picture. He felt he might be on the path to fame after that. Carl liked to read, and one of his favorite authors was Leo Busgaglia. Unbeknown to me, he began corresponding with the famous author. One day he matter of factly showed me a handwritten letter from Mr. Busgaglia, one of four he would receive over a period of eighteen months. Our hearts were warmed as we read his genuine words of love and encouragement. Here was a man who truly demonstrated God's love, taking time out of his busy schedule to correspond with our son.

From a letter dated April 13, 1993, I have included 3 paragraphs.

> Dear Carl,
>   Sometimes, with the many miles between us and the rest of the world that we want to love, all we can send is a prayer, a loving thought and/or some words of encouragement. Thank you for yours. You really put into practice what we both believe in.
>   With all my travels and activities it's been a long time since I've written...too long! I'm pleased to know that you had enjoyable holidays with your parents. I enjoyed mine with family and friends, too. I found your poem "Lost Forever" inspiring. It offers hope, help and a better tomorrow. As you say, it's up to us to create our own better tomorrow.
>   [His closing words of encouragement flowed:]
> Of course, I wish you a joyful spring. May you continue to grow in love and share it freely, for it is the only answer and our fundamental purpose.
>   Warmly,
>   Leo[1]

At age twenty-six, while Carl was still living with us, he made another bid for fame by engaging a newspaper reporter to take a picture of him sitting alongside an elaborate and colorful art collage he had created on the walls of our basement. Later, at age twenty-nine, another lengthy article and picture portrayed his life in a group home and reached a million readers through the newspaper's distribution. We had just celebrated his thirtieth birthday. He continued to seek out opportunities for fame. Two weeks before he died, he called us.

"Turn on channel 7 and watch the 6:00 p.m. news," he said excitedly. "I'm going to be on television."

We anxiously tuned in and saw him playing his violin in the downtown area. I recognized him immediately leaning against a light pole while playing his violin with great animation. I was so proud of him as I listened to the announcer shower him with accolades for his talent and sense of adventure.

But there was another part of life that was difficult for Carl. Under his brave smile and sensitive nature, he dealt with rejection and discrimination everywhere he went. His sense of self-worth would plummet when he lost a job or became psychotic. He seemed to lose a part of himself each time and had only his inner voices to comfort him.

When he took the medication Clozaril, the voices ceased, but he said to us, "I really miss not having my voices to talk to." No one could understand this cry of anguish except those of us who loved and cared for him. I knew how lonely he was without his voices. I think toward the end he just gave up trying to make sense of this life and needed to find some peace.

The weekend before he died, we went to pick him up at his group home but he wasn't there. We drove around the area, but he was no-

Carl, original collage, 1980.

where to be found. We had weekly standing date for dinner, so when he wasn't there we were puzzled that he hadn't let us know he couldn't meet us. When we returned home, I called and left him a message, but he didn't return our phone call. This behavior wasn't typical of him and left me with an uneasy, unsettled feeling. We missed our weekly chat with him and, at the time, didn't know we would never have the opportunity to be with him again.

Act of suicide

Two of his mental health team workers drove into our driveway on June 18, 1993, a date that will forever live in my memory.

Ward, standing outside, greeted them with, "What brings you here, coming all this way?" Their silence prompted Ward to say, "Carl's dead, isn't he?"

They nodded, "Yes, he died early this morning. He hanged himself in the basement of his home." Ward's head dropped to his chest as he emitted a heavy sigh. One of the workers asked, "Do you want us to tell your wife?"

Ward said, "No, no, I'd like to tell her myself."

I had a panicky feeling that something was wrong when Ward came into the house. He took my hand, his own trembling, and spoke those dreaded, piercing words,

"Oh, Mary, Carl's dead; he hanged himself last night."

"Oh my God. Oh, my sweet Carl, No, no!"

Once again, Ward and I embraced each other in our anguish over a beloved lost son and cried. The nightmare had recurred. Numb, we invited the team members in to tell us what had happened.

"It seems," they said, "that when Carl didn't show up for breakfast, one of the men went looking for him and found him in the basement." We pressed for the details.

"Carl was wearing his sweat pants, a T-shirt and he still had his glasses on," they shared.

I showed the team workers a picture of our four children, saying, "Here are our children when our daughters were eight and six, and our boys were four and two years old." I stared at their shining angelic faces as the picture took me temporarily back to that age of innocence. With reluctance, though, I put the picture down and returned to the gruesome present.

We now faced life without both Steve, who had died five years earlier at age twenty-seven and now Carl at age thirty. Lightning had struck twice.

I was plunged back into horrendous grief once again, this time for the loss of my youngest son. His tortured soul was now free to soar, but my earthbound burden was heavy. We had Carl's remains cremated, and his ashes placed in his brother's grave. Our boys were together in Heaven. We were alone on Earth.

Carl, life is good, 1992.

5

The Journey After Suicide

"Death does not exist."

Dr. Elisabeth Kübler-Ross[1]

Abandonment through suicide

Around the church, I saw hundreds of friends and family who had come to celebrate Carl's life. The congregation joined their voices in singing, "Joyful, Joyful, We Adore Thee," and I said to myself, *Thank you God for all these people who came to support us on this difficult day.* Music was an important part of Carl's life and played a significant role in his memorial service. Sitting in the sanctuary next to Ward, I felt mysteriously tranquil as if the sunlight, beaming images through the beautiful stained glass windows, were whispering comfort to me. As I listened to our friend play the majestic Moehler organ, I was reminded of my father, Carl's namesake, who had played this same instrument for twenty-five years. I also saw the image of my dad and me sitting on the bench as he patiently instructed me on how to play the pedals on the organ. Realizing I was daydreaming, I was quickly brought back to the service. I heard my brother and my niece each sing, and their beautiful voices brought tears as their songs touched my heart. I was uplifted by the minister's homily, speaking of Carl's struggles but with a note of humor to bring a touch of levity to our deep loss.

In the months that followed Carl's funeral, I was constantly in conversations that made me deal with the meaning of both my sons' actions. Suicide is like no other death. It is the ultimate form of abandonment.

According to the National Vital Statistics Report (2000),[2] every 43 seconds someone attempts suicide, and every eighteen minutes someone dies by suicide. But these facts alone are no solace to the grieving.

Suicide is defined as "the act of killing oneself intentionally."[3] The painful truth is that it only takes a moment in time for that to occur. It only took an instant for our sons to act upon their tortured mental states. But it takes much more than an instant for a mother to comprehend. Seeking that understanding would take me years of questioning. *Why did they do it? What could I have done differently? How do I ever find normalcy in my life again?* The hole was too large, the loss too great.

My religion, like most, would have us believe that because of one isolated action, our sons were sinful. To me, that didn't take into account all the years Steve and Carl were kind and compassionate, loving and caring. The public also buys into the stereotype that a person who completes suicide will spend eternity in hell.

I found myself rebelling against the religion in which I had been immersed all my life, a belief system which now crumbled around me. The rich words and dogma of my church became nothing more than religious platitudes that would send my sons to hell. Those words and phrases I had accepted without question rang pointlessly in my ears. After each cliché, the hypocrisy of the church began to explode in my mind.

You will have eternal life…if you don't take your own life.

Are you saved? Yes, you can be saved…if you don't commit suicide.

Is he a member of the church?…It's our chance to save him.

Is he a member in good standing? Does he believe…all the dogma we preach?

You will go to hell…if you don't believe our way.

I had heard many ministers preach exclusion rather than inclusion. This dogma of my church was limiting, uninspiring, and no longer resonated with my truth.

I was confused with these mixed messages and angry at God for allowing my sons to die. I was no longer sure if my prayers for strength and guidance to get through this profound loss were actually heard. *If God intervenes,* I asked myself, *where was He when Steve and Carl needed help? This is NOT God's will,* I argued with myself. *How can a God of love let this sort of anguish happen?*

I was an avid reader and resonated to what Marianne Williamson wrote, "True religion is internal, not external."[4] Also, in one of his sermons, the Catholic priest, Father Henri Nouwen, said, "Ideologies breed death; faith brings forth life."[5] I had more questions than answers, but I knew that one day the answers would be revealed to me. I also know that my sons' deaths robbed me of my innocence. I was not the same person anymore. I was totally humbled by Steve's and Carl's deaths, especially when I realized I was not in control of my life anymore than I had been of theirs. If I had any control, Steve and Carl would still be alive.

With death at my doorstep, I was consoled by my beloved husband who could look at the larger picture. With great compassion in this voice, he said to me, "Although I am in great pain over the death of Steve and Carl, Mary, we know that in death there is freedom. My joys lies in my belief that our sons are now freed from the limitations of time and a body, and they return to their original God-like state. All illusions of their physical lives fall away, and they aren't separated from us or from God."

If my sons had died of cancer, as tragic as that would have been, perhaps my search for meaning through my religion would have brought some sense of satisfaction, but the stigma of suicide doesn't allow for that. To my own astonishment, I found myself embarrassed, my ego bruised, buying into popular opinion and a religion that would tell me I was to blame.

I had to face, in a very public way with family, with friends, and with our congregation my own self doubts, my crumbling sense of self worth as a mother and as a minister's wife.

Early coping strategies that failed

In an attempt to deny my loss, my grief, and my public humiliation, I buried myself in the familiarity of a demanding work schedule. I found myself "burning the candle at both ends." There is always plenty of work to do at the university where I was assigned, not only my normal class load and supervision of the music therapy clinic, but I also became the department volunteer eager to fill every void. I soon found myself involved again in state, regional and national professional activities, all designed to keep my mental activity diverted from my pain. At the time, I was unaware that my workaholism was a coping device that helped me gain strength to turn back once again to a path of deeper healing. This was a time during which I developed a renewed sense of worth and self-confidence through my successes and the support of an academic environment. The joy of teaching lifted my spirits as I experienced with my students their energy and enthusiasm for learning which rekindled my own.

Ward and I sought the professional help of a psychologist whom Steve had actually seen once before he died. From this intervention, I became aware of my feelings of denial, guilt, fear, and anger and began to have insights into patterns that weren't supportive of my emotional wellness. It was my first wake-up call to emotions safely buried that now wanted to surface. My inner critic was protecting me as I felt my resistance build. To avoid my fear, I put blame on others which only strengthened my evasion. My first assignment was to allow those fears to surface and to listen to the message. I found that my most brutal critic was the one that taunted me by saying, "You're not good enough." I began to journal, but I was only scratching the surface of my feelings. I didn't have the energy or the will to change.

My therapy took a step backwards when, soon after Steve died, the psychologist revealed some unexpected and shocking news. "I have some important information I'd like to share with you," she said apologetically. "I wasn't free to communicate this with you before Steve died since our patient/therapist confidentiality had to be respected."

"Yes," what is it?" I said with some anxiety.

"Steve had been taking cocaine while he was in California."

I asked myself, Why, why, why? Why had he become addicted to such a deadly substance, and why hadn't this trained professional seen the signs of a possible suicide? My doubt in the psychologist's skill loomed large. I was angry with her. I had trusted her to evaluate my son's condition and help him in his need.

My emotions were raw, and I struggled through moments of depression. For months after Steve's death, I replayed conversations he and I had had during the last few days of his life.

"You seem sad, Steve," I'd said. "What's wrong?"

He replied in a quiet and low voice, "I just can't concentrate anymore."

"Would you like to talk to a psychologist?" I knew I was treading on sensitive ground.

"No, not right now," he replied. "I'll be okay."

I felt so helpless and sad to see him that way. I revisited every word and expression and tried to think how it might have been different. It was the only way for me to process and eventually realize the futility of those thoughts. Finally, I had to accept that nothing—no conversation, prayer or tears—could ever bring him back. With this final recognition and acceptance, I sobbed until my whole body ached.

Ward, in turn, was working on some of his own fear issues. We had hoped we would never need the psychologist's services again, but Ward made an appointment with her six months after Steve's death. Bouts of recurring diarrhea, stomach problems, and the heart-rending picture of Steve hanging from the rafters kept him from sleeping. The psychologist, who was trained in Neuro-Linguistic Programming (NLP), a behavioral technology that allows you to change, adopt or eliminate behaviors, assured Ward this technique would help him get rid of the horrendous vision of Steve. Ward was instructed to see the picture of Steve hanging from the rafters in black and white and reduce the picture to its smallest frame, until it disappeared. Then he was asked to think of a special time he had shared with Steve where they were happy together. Ward visualized Steve and himself on Father's Day laughing and joking around, and Steve's handing him a gift. He saw this picture in vivid color and was told to make it as large as he could. Then, the psychologist gave him an anchor on his right "pinky" finger which he would touch every time he thought of Steve. Much to his surprise and relief, each time he did this, he could see only the colored picture of Steve and him sharing a joyful experience. The negative vision was gone. His diarrhea and stomach problems subsided, and he was able to get a full night's sleep again.

To add to our stress, Ward's brother, Don, called to tell us about his encounter with his co-worker. Out of curiosity, Ward asked, "What happened?"

"Well," Don said hesitantly, "my co-worker struck up a conversation with me to offer condolences for Steve's death." " That was considerate," Ward replied.

"I was surprised but pleased at first, that he took time to talk to me, but then the conversation changed dramatically."

"What do you mean, Don?" "I mean," he said, with a lot of emotion in his voice, "I mean, he looked me in the eye and said, 'You know your nephew is going to hell.' I was flabbergasted, and my first reaction was to punch the guy in the mouth, but instead, I walked away furious at his ignorance and intolerance."

Ward had no words to describe his anger and disappointment.

There were other occasions on which Ward experienced people's unkind words and actions. In the workplace, my colleagues were there for me when I needed a smile and reassurance. When Ward showed any irritation in his church job, people seemed offended. They acted as if they expected him to minister to them as if nothing was going on in his own personal life. The pastor is not allowed to have feet of clay, to feel or experience the same emotions as his flock. Who ministers to the minister?

No one seemed able to understand that Ward couldn't fully minister to them because of his own unresolved grief. I, on the other hand was there to support him through his difficult time, and he was there for me. Through our mutual support of each other, our bond grew stronger and more durable.

Insights into my denial

In the meantime, I was gaining the strength I needed to begin to face how my workaholism kept me in denial. I have spent most of my life in denial of one kind or another. From the time I was a child, I denied my father's alcoholism. We needed to project the image of the "perfect family;" and, as a family defense against the truth, I denied emotions. If there had been an elephant in our living room, no one would have mentioned it. We didn't talk about feelings, my father, or our fears. I lived by the rules and wishes of my parents in denial of my own. I learned to deny my own self, and I carried this into my adult life.

Though I learned to share when I met my future husband, Ward, at age thirteen, my pattern of denial was already set. He struggled to get me to open up and share my feelings in total honesty. I was afraid I wouldn't be "perfect," that I would be judged, that I had done something wrong or that my thoughts were crazy. Why should I risk being put down and feeling the familiar pain of never being quite good enough?

Denial is linked closely to control, which I had to have as "super mom." I had to take care of everything; and, though the positive side of that became the fabric of our family, the negative side of needing to stay in control kept me from being vulnerable. I had developed my mother's stoic heart, and I needed to learn softness and the ability to give and receive demonstrative signs of love.

My work and my life patterns certainly kept me in a state of denial through my initial stages of grief. I held on to them dearly, for I knew nothing else. I wasn't willing to accept signals that did come my way to help me, including the protective barrier I had wrapped myself in. I turned to food to fill the void. Though I had noticed a weight gain over the years, I found ways to deny the root cause with palatable excuses for adding pounds.

Seeking control, avoiding risks, and low self-worth are all aspects which foster denial. So is giving away personal power. In not feeling honored as a child, I became an adult who sought recognition, but felt fear at its presence. I felt unworthy and embarrassed when attention was directed my way, while at a deeper level I was crying out for the recognition and love I deserved but hadn't the self-esteem to accept.

And when my sons died, all my buried denials came up full-force to challenge me.

I needed to see the roots of these issues and problems and understand them as patterns everyone has in their lives. I had to confront my denial once and for all.

When I lost Steve and Carl, I denied my part. I denied the guilt I felt at not always being a good role model for open communication, and the normal guilt that goes along with being a parent. I felt ashamed over not wanting to be with my sons when their schizophrenia brought out bizarre behaviors. These incidents threatened my efforts to keep the public image of normalcy in the face of judgments that would have my sons, my family, and me labeled differently. I also felt guilty about being upset with Carl when, taking him out for dinner, he wore his weird outfits of a trench coat and a do-rag on his head. Another pang of guilt kept surfacing about having asked Steve to live in an apartment instead of allowing him to continue living at home. Then there was my denial in dismissing his diagnosis of mental illness as a temporary reaction to the stress of living as a homeless person.

I was devastated when Carl decided to take his life despite his promise to me that he wouldn't. However, another part of me was relieved he no longer had to endure the insidious illness of schizophrenia. My grieving process was different this time, or so I thought. I had mourned so deeply for so long after Steve's death, it somehow seemed unnecessary to access that pain again. I rationalized that, because Carl had attempted suicide several times and suffered from the effects of schizophrenia for thirteen long years, I knew it might eventually happen. That fall, however, I came down with a severe case of pneumonia. *I wonder if this is a result of not allowing myself to grieve properly over Carl's death,* I pondered. It felt as if I needed to go inside myself and release my repressed anger and sadness, yet I resisted for fear of what I might uncover.

Expressing anger

Part of my healing process was learning to express my anger appropriately. I realized I was directing my anger inward, and I felt out of control. I began using profanity when I was fearful, angry or frustrated. Since that wasn't my usual modus operandi, heads turned as I expressed myself vehemently. I took to screaming into a pillow and hitting the bed with a tennis racket as well as working out in an aerobics class and riding my bike. While enrolled as a psychodrama trainer, I broke my toe while kicking a ball and yelling at Carl for putting me through this pain. My efforts at dissipating my pent-up energy worked temporarily; however, my biggest challenge was to express verbally what I was feeling at the moment.

In the early years of our marriage, Ward and I communicated as well as we knew how, which at best wasn't truly effective. My style was to stuff my anger and delay discussing my issues with Ward, while his technique was to vent his anger easily and openly, get it all out, and deal with it. We usually reached a frustrating impasse since neither of us knew how to get our needs met in a healthy way. Now we look back in dismay at the monumental effort it took to understand each other.

We began bravely to look at our issues of needing to control one another's behavior. For instance, while typing one of Ward's sermons I altered the wording of a sentence I thought needed some grammatical changes. On Sunday morning, as he looked down to read that sentence, he stumbled over the wording. I clearly realized then that my lesson was not to manipulate his manuscript to meet my standards. Indeed, he and I express ourselves differently and that's just fine. I quickly apologized, and he graciously accepted my regrets.

Ingrained response patterns don't just magically go away. We both grew tired of the stalemates; but, instead of retreating farther from each other as many couples do under stress, we chose instead to look at the fear that held us back from communicating our bona fide feelings to each other. We were ready to rediscover our true selves, the beautiful selves hidden under all the defensive layers. As I allowed myself to be aware of my fears and began expressing them to Ward, he began to look at himself too.

Soon after we began sharing our feelings, he said "I feel so close to you when we share our intimate secrets with each other."

We were both beginning to move into a healthier place of communication and understanding each other and ourselves better.

I've learned throughout our growing together as a couple that expectations are nothing more than control issues. I criticized Ward for what I thought he should say or do. His control issues, on the other hand, involved telling me what to do and that he wanted me to know he was "the man of the house." When we acted this way, we dishonored each other and ourselves. The process of rediscovering who we really are began as we each took responsibility for communicating clearly and honestly.

Robert Camp, author of the book, *Love Cards*, says, "When we are in love, everything within us that is unloving or fearful is forced to come to the surface to be dealt with."[6] As partners, Ward and I are mirrors for each other. As we began to repattern old, stuck behaviors, we were able to change our thought forms and communication habits, which in turn freed us both to accept each other as we are.

Now, when we get upset with each other, we have the skill to talk out our misunderstandings, clear the air, and move on quickly. We don't play the old games or tapes as much as we used to.

Learning forgiveness

Another major ingredient for understanding one another is forgiveness, of self and of others. The Course of Miracles states that forgiveness is the key to happiness.[7] I realize that I am my own worst enemy when it comes to making a mistake, and I only hurt myself with my harsh judgments. Recently I took a wrong turn while driving to an important appointment. Because I read the map wrong I was late. Usually I would dwell on how stupid I was for letting that happen. Instead, I forgave myself, and I felt free from my self-inflicted punishment. I took back my power.

As for forgiving others, sometimes I harbored resentments and fed my bruised pride. Even when Ward and I were barely keeping our life together during the strain of our sons' deaths, we realized we each had only the other for support. It was my misguided expectation that someone would reach out to us in our time of grief. Yet few understood our problems, and even fewer bothered to find out how to help ease the tremendous strain that weighed us down. I needed to forgive them and myself. I went to several friends who I thought had ignored me in my pain and told them that it was my fear, not their actions, that was responsible for my being upset. I chose to be happy instead of right. This admission cleared the air, and in that spirit of forgiveness, we remain good friends.

Outside support

I know that most people are uncomfortable in the face of grief. Dr. Mitsuo Aoki, a professor at the University of Hawaii, speaking on the subject of Death and Dying, was once asked in a seminar how to approach a friend who was dying of cancer. "I don't know what to say to her," the woman lamented.

Dr. Aoki asked quietly, "What would you say to your friend if she weren't dying of cancer? Just say those things."[8]

Still, for the average person, words are hard to come by. I now know mourning over loss is a personal journey that is healed only by trusting the inner voice of God within.

Four months after Carl's death, we organized a Survivors of Suicide group (SOS), established for people who have lost loved ones through the act of suicide. The format was modeled after a group in Grand Rapids, Michigan, because of the help and caring Ward and I had received in the course of attending several meetings there after Steve's death.

Feelings ran high at our first meeting as people came together, grieving from their recent loss. Ward and I greeted them warmly and hugged those who granted permission. Some wept, and some remained stoic anticipating this new group encounter.

Meeting once a month to talk about our loved ones in a safe space freed me to articulate my feelings. No judgments were placed on us. Group members supported and sustained each other through the difficult first year after the suicide of our loved ones, especially through holidays, their birthdays, and the anniversary date of their deaths. The closer it came to Steve's birthday, the larger the knots in my stomach became. I dreaded turning the calendar over to May 31. My personal pain was so intense, I didn't know how I would get through it. I felt so alone. No one called to tell me they were thinking about me or him on that horrible day, and even Ward didn't want to be reminded of the pain. Steve's birth was such a beautiful part of my life and now it was another painful day. That first year I lit a candle for him on what would have been his twenty-eighth birthday, and told him I loved him. As I relived both the joys and the sorrow of so many significant family events, I felt my heart break over and over again. This helped me see that I needed a change in traditional family rituals. Now on special dates, Ward and I now make our sons' favorite mixture of chocolate chips and walnuts and take it to the cemetery where we sprinkle the concoction over the boys' grave. It has helped us deal more effectively with the yearly reminder of our loss.

Several of us in the SOS group had been faced with the situation in which someone asks, "How many children do you have?" We all agreed we felt strong emotions when that question arose. We all shared our experiences.

"I base my response on how I feel at the moment," I confessed, "and I check in with my gut to see whether I am strong enough to explain the boys' deaths. Soon after their deaths I would say 'We have four children,' hoping they wouldn't ask me about each child. As time went on I said, 'We had four children. Our daughters are in New Hampshire and California, but our sons died several years ago.' One day I heard Ward say, 'We have two daughters on this side and our sons are on the other side.' That caused a bit more reaction as people tried to comprehend what he was saying. Now I often reply, 'We have two daughters, but our two sons died by suicide several years ago.' Often that brings out people's judgment and although some don't want me to know they are shocked, I can see it in their faces. I am open in saying Steve and Carl took their own lives because it is a way to connect with others who have had a loved one die by suicide. But on my vulnerable days, I still choose to say, 'We have two daughters,' and stop there. I take care of myself and let others do the same."

Other support

Ward and I thank God for people who care. We are so fortunate to have many compassionate friends and caring family members who helped us through our grieving by sharing kind deeds and stories of our sons. My sister and brother-in-law and Ward's brother and his wife volunteered to remove Carl's belongings from his room, a task I couldn't bear to face. On his bed lay the bloodstained quilt I had made him. I asked my sister to throw it away. It held too many sad memories.

Another thoughtful demonstration of caring was the planting of a tree at our cottage in memory of Steve and Carl by their cousins, a sweet tradition we carried on as we moved from place to place, always planting a tree in remembrance of them.

Telephone calls and stories about how our sons touched other's lives were very helpful to our healing process. We received a call from a young man that touched our hearts. He told us this story. "Last summer a young man came by our house every few days while my son and I were remodeling the front porch. He would stop and ask if it was okay to sit down on the steps and talk. He had a sensitive spirit and a gentle sense of humor, and we looked forward to his visits. He never stayed long, but always had some kind word to say about how the work on the porch was progressing, and then he'd bid us goodbye and continue his walk. I have to admit I didn't pay much attention to him but listened as I worked. It wasn't until your niece called and told me that Carl lived in this neighborhood that I realized this kind visitor was your son." The stranger continued his story, his voice choking up as he said, "I feel so badly I missed an opportunity to know Carl better. It is a bitter-sweet illustration for me that everyone who appears in my life has a lesson for me. I will be more sensitive to the next person who comes into my life." When he identified himself, he was not a stranger to Ward and me, but a young man who had been in our church youth group.

We received an especially poignant letter from a young man who wrote, "I met Steve at church camp, and I owe my life to him. I want you to know that it was Steve's loving words and friendship that helped me conquer my depression. Because of his influence, I accepted the Spirit of God into my life."

Also especially healing was my conversation with Steve's friend from high school, who had driven 300 miles to attend the funeral. This young man had tears in his eyes as he recalled the fun and laughter he and Steve had shared in marching band and in other music experiences in school.

Shortly after Carl's death we received this letter from Leo Busgaglia.[9]

Aug. 17, 1993

Dear Rev. Ward and Mary,

Thank you for writing and sharing the very sad news concerning your son's suicide. As you can imagine, since I value life, love and happiness so much, I was greatly saddened.

Through our correspondence I came to know the same warmth, compassion, sensitivity and humor you wrote of. I know he loved you very much and mentioned his family often in his letters.

I wish I had words adequate to comfort you in your time of grief. Life is such a precious gift of God, one that few of us would be willing to reject. How tragic that the mental illness Carl had fought against so bravely gained the upper hand.

We will all surely miss him. And we will all have to work a little harder to fill his void. His memory will always live in my heart.

Warmly,
Leo

Moving to the light

My journey began with glimpses of mere bits of Light that helped me through the early stages of grief. The Light reveals itself as an awakening which evolves into an awareness of love's presence in my life. It is there to encourage me to find out who I really am.

As I stripped my resistance to the childhood patterns that had brought about the lifelong root causes of my denial, I knew I needed to dig deeper. What I had learned was important but not sufficient. I had addressed my anger and frustration at my sons' mental illness and the ensuing problems with the mental health system. I had grown in my understanding that the stigma of suicide is one I would only wear by choice, and there was nothing I could do to change the finality of death. My lifetime soul mate eased that journey, and yet I knew I had more to learn to find the peace that remained elusive. I still sought the Light within. Although I thought I had surrendered to the dark night of my soul at the time of Steve's death, I later learned that I had to go deeper into the darkness to come through finally to the Light.

When Ward and I moved to Oklahoma in 1995, that descent into the darkness began. We set out happily to begin a new adventure so Ward could complete his doctorate. I went with plans to leave behind the academic life and find new challenges with a sound therapy business. The first year was a joyful and exciting time for us.

We chose to live in a spiritual community based on a metaphysical philosophy. Approximately 200 people lived on the mountainside outside the city in a single family residential setting. Central to this community were a seminary, a church and a wellness center, which drew, in addition to residential members, a constant stream of students who came to prepare for the ministry.

I decided to take classes, and I became involved as the director of the church music program. That first year I found new strength in the camaraderie of like-minded seekers and I continued to heal. Both Ward and I became involved and invested in building future capacity and sustainability for a growing spiritual program to which both of us felt highly committed.

The second year, however, we began to feel more disenchanted with the inevitable fact that all organizations have a downside of bureaucracy. Though we had built a new home, we couldn't deny that the once strong commitment was beginning to wane. We knew we needed to move on.

We settled in Arkansas, a place in which our ministry was facilitating a Sunday morning fellowship and helping to develop a spiritual center. I began a music therapy business to help people heal through the use of music and sound.

Two years later, we became restless once more, and an opportunity opened up for us to live in Hawaii. Having visited the Hawaiian Islands several times in four years, we felt an affinity to the land, to the Hawaiian culture, to the traditions, and to the ancestors. We meticulously wrote down the pros and cons of moving to an island so far out in the Pacific Ocean. The "for" list outweighed the "against" list by far, so we made a decision to move.

We called our daughters and told them they could have their inheritance now because we had decided to sell everything they didn't want and move to Hawaii. They were amazed, yet supportive. In record time, we sold our house, had a huge garage sale, gave our books to our center, shipped furniture to Marcia in New Hampshire, pulled a U-Haul to California to drop off furniture to Kathy, and drove our car to San Francisco to be shipped to Hawaii. We treated ourselves to a first class flight. After all, we were going to live in paradise. A few days after we arrived we unpacked our twenty-six boxes, the extent of our material possessions. We were mobile, with nothing to tie us down. We settled into a new life in paradise not realizing that this is where the next level of healing would occur.

The next level of healing

My inner work began soon after we arrived in Hawaii. I was ready to release the last remnants of my grieving. It was time to get back to writing the book that I had begun two years previously. I had put it away for a year or so, not wanting to access my unresolved pain. Now, while I had a support group of loving friends and my husband there for me, once again I peeled away another layer of defenses and fears. I cried as I meditated and acknowledged feelings that had been repressed. I sobbed as I sat at my computer expressing my feelings of pain. But each time I went deeper inside, I felt lighter and more joyful. Completing my book was a major breakthrough into feeling a sense of peace and accomplishment.

Life today

After two years, we were ready to move again, back to the mainland. We missed being close to our children and grandchildren. We settled in South Carolina where we presently live and are very content.

Since retiring, we are in each other's company twenty-four hours a day. Talk about a test of a relationship! Both of us read a lot, so we always have much to share with each other. We share insights we get during our morning meditations, and we respect each other's boundaries. We operate on spontaneity, always ready to go and do something different every day.

Ward says, "Life has become joyful, pleasurable, and filled with inner wisdom. We allow ourselves to be 'led by the Spirit of the God within.' It's like giving birth. Our sacred mission led Mary to the adventure of writing a book; I established a wedding business while together we share in a spiritual fellowship."

I view our long-term relationship as having brought me insights instead of problems and failures, things to be learned and understood. Through thick and thin, we both have learned to love ourselves.

In the midst of it all, we are best friends. We feel blessed to have great relationships with our daughters and sons-in-law, and we love our wonderful grandchildren, Dylan, Kayla, Devi, and our "adopted" granddaughter, Chris. We enjoy traveling, reading, swimming in the Atlantic ocean, the company of good friends, uplifting spiritual conversations, good movies, and best of all, making love.

We are not only surviving, but thriving.

Ward and Mary, soulmates, 2003

6

Dealing With The Mental Health System

"Patients wander our streets, lost in time, as if in a medieval city. We are protecting their civil liberties much more adequately than we are protecting their minds and their lives."[1]

Lloyd M. Siegel, *The New York Times*, 1981

Learning of our youngest son's illness

The first indication that Carl was having problems appeared when he was a senior in high school. Within a year of securing treatment for him, the psychologist recommended that Carl see a psychiatrist. It was becoming evident that Carl needed medication, so we made an appointment with a doctor who was highly regarded in his field. After examining our son, he gave us his assessment. I will never forget his harsh words. "Carl will never be well."

I sat paralyzed in disbelief. After disbelief came anger. I was determined to prove him wrong.

Fortunately, our naiveté kept us from knowing we were standing precariously on the edge of a dark abyss; and, if we looked away, even for a moment, we would easily tumble into the void. It was difficult for Carl, as well as the rest of the family, to admit he had a mental illness. After enduring this hideous chemical imbalance of the brain for many years, Carl cried, "This disease sucks." I thought it did, too.

Can any of us imagine how confusing and paralyzing it must be to have a brain that doesn't function? If we haven't "walked in those moccasins," we can't fully understand.

Although his behavior was confusing to me and to our family, at times he appeared emotionally healthy and stable and was able to make decisions for himself. However, when his illness reached an acute or psychotic phase, he couldn't think logically and lost all sense of himself and others. As I witnessed his change in behavior, I grew more and more bewildered and began searching for resources and information to help me understand this peculiar illness.

Schizophrenia

Schizophrenia is a neurological brain disorder and is believed to be the single most destructive disease to young people. Of the five to six million people in the United States currently diagnosed with mental illness, one to two million people—*or one in everyone hundred Americans*—have been diagnosed with schizophrenia. Most cases develop between the ages of seventeen and twenty-five.

E. Fuller Torrey, M.D., author of *Surviving Schizophrenia*, calls schizophrenia "a cruel disease."[2] The American Psychiatric Association describes it as "one of the most debilitating and baffling mental illnesses known."[3] Years of research has shown that schizophrenia is a biologically-based brain disease. Brain imaging has confirmed imbalances of two brain chemicals—dopamine and serotonin.[4]

Torrey in, *Surviving Schizophrenia*, says that schizophrenia is not:
— caused by childhood trauma;
— caused by domineering mothers and/or passive fathers;
— caused by any guilts, acts, or failures of the victim: or
— responsive to treatment by psychotherapy

Rather, he contends, schizophrenia:
— is a real disease (or group of diseases);
— does have concrete and specific symptoms different from other mental illnesses;
— is a result of flawed brain biochemistry;
— may be treatable by specific psychotropic drugs;
— often has a genetic component; and, most importantly,
— is sometimes curable.[5]

Contrary to popular belief, schizophrenia is not a "split personality." The vast majority of people who suffer from schizophrenia are not at all dangerous to others.

Torrey strongly believes "schizophrenia is in fact the single biggest blemish on the face of contemporary American medicine and social services: when the social history of our era is written, the plight of persons with schizophrenia will be recorded as having been a national scandal."[6]

One symptom of schizophrenia is over-acuteness of the senses, the blunting of sensations where a person may not feel pain. In one of his psychotic states, Carl used a knife to carve a cross in his arm. When I saw it, I was alarmed and said, "Oh, Carl, that must hurt you terribly," but he reassured me saying, "Don't worry, Mom, it doesn't hurt at all."

On a day-to-day basis, Carl barely coped with his symptoms, nor did I. I felt my stress level rise as I stood by, helplessly watching him function the best he could. His struggle to think clearly caused him to be agitated and hindered his ability to make good choices. While he would try to fend off the voices that gave him the negative messages and hallucinations, their presence in his mind caused him to withdraw and become apathetic. Because of these symptoms so commonly associated with schizophrenia, he had difficulty relating to others appropriately. This negatively impacted upon his ability to take the initiative to find employment. Steve, too, manifested some of these symptoms the last few months of his life. Watching them struggle, I only hoped it would go away. I could never rest because of the unpredictable nature of this illness.

Medication

It was common for Carl to go off his medication. *Physicians' Reference Book*7 describes the numerous unpleasant side effects of each anti-psychotic drug. As a result of his medication, Carl would experience dizziness, dry mouth, constipation, blurred vision, drowsiness, slurred speech, and tremors of his hands, to name just a few. Is it any wonder he wasn't compliant?

It took constant attention to keep him stabilized on his medication. I had become all too familiar with the consequences of conventional anti-psychotic drugs such as Haldol (haloperiodol), Stelazine (trifluoperazine), and Prolixin (fluphenazine) and I knew which anti-psychotic drugs worked for him and which had debilitating side effects.

Symptoms common among psychotropic drugs are insomnia, headache, anxiety, agitation, and extra pyramidal symptoms such as muscle stiffness, tremors, and body shakes. As if these aren't enough, more significant side effects can include low blood pressure, sleepiness, constipation, heart palpitations, sexual dysfunction, weight gain, and dizziness.

Other drugs were also prescribed. He was given Cogentin and Artane, designed to reduce or eliminate stiffness and tremors. These drugs also have side effects of their own. Being on psychotropic drugs too long can cause tardive dyskinesia (TD), which manifests in symptoms such as grimacing, smacking of lips, sucking, and other spasmodic involuntary movements. Carl was also taking Lithium, which is used to reduce wide mood swings. By-products of this drug can include nausea, vomiting, diarrhea, abdominal cramps, muscle weakness or tremor, thirst, frequent urination, tiredness, and weight gain. Most of these side effects are related to the level of the drug in the bloodstream. Carl had his blood levels checked weekly at first, then monthly. The most noticeable side effects were tremors in his hands and his gradual weight gain.

It seems that dispensing drugs is all anyone expects of our mental health system; however, to a parent involved in a child's treatment, one finds out quickly the fallacy of the promises of drug treatment.

Carl went off his medication due to the unbearable side effects. It became apparent that he needed to be hospitalized to stabilize his erratic behavior.

Hospitalization

He was first hospitalized at a private psychiatric facility located only thirty minutes from our home. Ward and I drove through the sprawling campus with ponds, walking trails, and many auspicious looking buildings and finally found the admission building. We were informed of the hospital's excellent "milieu" therapy, a five-day-a-week intense program which focused on the patient's problems. We were assured they were staffed with a team of outstanding nurses and psychiatrists as well as their expanding psychotherapy program, a residency program, and innumerable social and educational activities. We soon became acquainted with the hospital routine and requirements after Carl was locked up on a psychiatric unit and was assigned to a room with three other males. When we approached the unit during visiting hours, the staff would look through a small window at us to see who wanted to enter their "inner sanctum," the psychiatric unit. I bought into the myth that this respected institution would have the knowledge and expertise to cure my son's illness, but in fact that didn't happen. After Carl appeared totally listless and zombie-like during our first visit with him, we reported this incident to the social worker, after which the psychiatrist on staff was fired. The bill came to $60,000 for three months of treatment, including medication and activities, which, incidentally, was paid by our private insurance. Although Carl found relief from his psychotic break, it felt like mental illness was a death sentence, and no one understood it better than the patients and their families. The staff, although friendly, knew that this unit was a holding tank until the patients experienced another psychotic episode. When Carl was discharged, we had high hopes of his beating this illness.

The blaming game

One of my frustrations with the mental health system was the narrow way in which the professionals saw illness. While Carl was being evaluated for his first hospitalization, I was called into the social worker's office to be interviewed. I was questioned at length as to Carl's behavior and for information about our family. The questions didn't bother me as much as the attitude in which they were asked. I felt so violated as they fired questions at me. It felt biased and discriminatory. They really didn't want to hear my side of Carl's story. In the 1980's, no one recognized schizophrenia as a chemical imbalance in the brain; it was assumed to be all psychological. Professionals in the mental health field seemed to be looking for someone or something to blame it on; and, in my vulnerable state, I felt their accusations were directed at me. There was no mention of the father's involvement. Mental illness was definitely the mother's fault!

Two social workers pummeled me with questions. "Tell us about Carl's birth. Was it normal?"

"It was a normal premature birth," I retorted. "He was born seven weeks early however he weighed four pounds, eight ounces and was a very healthy baby boy." There was silence so I continued. "He spent the first four weeks of his life in an incubator, and I visited him every day at the hospital. My heart ached having to leave him there." Eyes glued to their yellow pads they wrote down every word I spoke. "I love Carl," I said, and he had a 'normal' life before the onset of this debilitating illness. Would you like to hear all the wonderful things about him?" I asked. More silence. I was upset because they seemed interested only in his weaknesses, not his strengths. They also questioned me about Ward's and my relationship and our connection to our children.

I left feeling resentful and dejected: I was to blame for my child's dysfunctional behavior. I hated the mental health system. I hated everything it stood for because it meant I had to look at a part of our family that was sick. I had never considered our family as dysfunctional or sick, yet here I was involved in a system that seemed to be looking for scapegoats. This was the system with which I was entrusting my child.

For the eight years that Carl lived with us, I became drained of energy trying to balance my professional life with his hospitalizations. Ward and I bought a duplex a few blocks from our home so he could live independently. Though his housing needs were met, he was still dependent upon us for his social, emotional, and financial needs. At this time we had to make one of the biggest decisions of our lives. In order for Carl to be truly independent of us, he would need to go on disability. With my background in mental health, I had some knowledge about obtaining services, but I soon discovered securing professional help for our son was like walking blindfolded through a dark maze.

I sent for brochures about the Michigan mental health system to help me in my quest for services. We received a packet of general information. In Michigan, the community mental health centers provide emergency assessment and services, community placement, medical supervision and treatment, and case management services for the mentally ill in the community. They are responsible for the mentally ill after they've been discharged from the hospital back into the community. How well these services are disbursed depends upon state funding, the employers, and the employees.[8]

Trying to get into the system

The fact was, in order to be accepted into the mental health system, there were several steps to take. The first was to contact a psychiatrist. Necessary paperwork that would qualify Carl for disability needed to be filled out. I knew whom to call, although I was reluctant to do so. The psychiatrist, who several months earlier had unsympathetically told us Carl would need this kind of treatment, was willing to help admit Carl in the system. I was happy I hadn't burned any bridges.

The next step was to go to the Social Security Office. I was ill the day Ward accompanied Carl to help him fill out the dreaded paperwork for two federal programs: SSI (Supplementary Security Income) and SSDI (Social Security Disability Income). The lines were long, and the atmosphere was bleak and oppressive. People of all ages, races, and cultures were mingling around the room trying to find answers to their many questions. Ward and Carl made the best of a dismal situation by telling jokes to each other. Finally, after securing the right papers, Ward quickly learned some important facts about these programs which are designed to provide a guaranteed annual income to the disabled, including the mentally ill. Staring at the papers, Ward read, "Disability is defined as 'an inability to engage in any substantial gainful activity by reason of any medically determined physical or mental impairment, which has lasted, or can be expected to last, for a continuous period of not less than twelve months.'"[9] So far, it described Carl's situation perfectly. It also stated that eligibility is assessed by the person's assets and other income along with: 1) evidence of a restriction of daily activities and interests, 2) deterioration in personal habits, 3) marked impairment in relating to other people, and 4) the inability to concentrate and carry out instructions necessary to hold a job. Carl had experienced all of these indicators.

Out of this gruesome experience came a spark of light when Carl was informed he could keep his car. As long as his assets weren't worth more than $2,500, he remained eligible. Another guideline of the system stated if he made more than $65 a month from his job, his SSI payment would be reduced.

After waiting impatiently for the dehumanizing system to compute all the information, we finally heard, one snowy day in Michigan, that Carl had qualified for benefits. We were shocked to read that his monthly income from SSI was only $425. Out of that minuscule sum, he was expected to pay rent, food, and all personal items. Payments are also reduced by one-third when the person lives at home. We questioned how he would make ends meet. Obviously, that was our problem, not theirs.

Once Carl received SSI income, we were relieved of some of the financial burden; however, we subsidized him every month so he could have some extras in his life. This was the first time we had dealt with any federal assistance, and we found the process demoralizing.

The third and final big step was to petition the mental health system for acceptance into the program. To our dismay, we learned that Carl wouldn't be accepted until he had been hospitalized three times. We threw up our hands in despair at the irony, realizing Carl had to become psychotic and hospitalized one more time before being admitted into the mental health system.

Acceptance into the mental health system

After meeting the required third hospitalization, Carl's petition was re-activated, and he qualified for the program. He was immediately assigned to a case manager whose job it was to help him with his daily living skills, provide job training, and monitor his medication.

The mental health system categorizes and compartmentalizes people according to how ill they appear to be at the time of admittance, so there are many holes in the system. Management for the severely ill primarily includes hospitalization and medication. A person who is "high functioning" and needs on-going services often falls through the cracks of the system. Carl was considered high functioning because he could hold down a job and take care of his own personal needs. The professionals assured us they would monitor his progress.

We communicated, at regular intervals, with the team manager and occasionally attended team meetings. When we were accused by them of being too involved in his treatment, I became defensive. If we didn't care about our son, who would? Nine years of living with the symptoms and cycles of his illness, we were very familiar with how schizophrenia affected our son. It felt as if his team members patronized us as we shared our perception of Carl's challenges. We agreed, however, that Carl's stubborn nature and his reluctance to attend group meetings were problems. Carl's interpretation was, "All that talk therapy doesn't help."

I was grateful to the case managers who checked up on him in his group home to see that he was taking his medication on a daily basis, getting to work on time and tending to personal hygiene. After each of his three suicide attempts, he was placed in a crisis home until he became stabilized, then sent back to his group home and his job.

Knowing the limitation that drugs placed on his illness, the search for an alternative treatment program seemed the solution. After his experience in California proved unsuccessful, Carl had no other choice but to return to the mental health system he had left. We were all very disappointed and disillusioned that what had at first seemed to be a perfect solution for Carl to be healed of schizophrenia, had turned out to be a disaster.

Fortunately, the mental health system in Michigan had an opening in their program; and, as they promised, Carl was assigned yet another case manager. They arranged for him to attend a program which would lead to employment. I was grateful they welcomed him back; but he, to the contrary, wasn't happy at starting over again with the same plan he had once completed.

Head down and in a depressed tone of voice, Carl said to me one day, "I feel like committing suicide."

I was furious! I said, "Carl, talk to your counselor. I just can't deal with that. Please don't say that to me again. I feel your despair, but it's very hard for me to hear you talk about suicide, especially after Steve's death. If you decide to end your life, I will be heartsick and devastated, but I can't follow you around. Carl, will you please talk to your counselor about your feelings?" He said he would.

We received a call from Carl's team worker advising that a change in medication was recommended for Carl because his current medication wasn't helping alleviate his symptoms any longer. They felt Carl was a good candidate for Clozaril, an atypical anti-psychotic drug. They told us it would cause a decrease in production of white blood cells, therefore his blood would have to be monitored every two weeks. Ward and I talked with Carl about the pros and cons of taking this new medication. After Carl decided to take Clozaril, his "voices" disappeared. His thinking became very clear, and I thought this might be the magic bullet that would be effective. One evening, though, Carl called to tell me he missed his "voices," and he was lonely and had no one to talk to. Again, I felt his sadness and frustration, but encouraged him to give the new drug more of a chance.

In only a matter of weeks, Carl died by suicide. We asked ourselves: had he become too clear about his possible prognosis? I will never know. It was as if another bomb had exploded, shattering small pieces of me once more. To lose a second child was incomprehensible. Deep down, I felt a sense of relief that Carl was finally free of his mental tortures; however, then I had to forgive myself for the guilt I suffered about feeling relief that Carl was dead.

It was hard to get past the initial promise of his recovery. At first he had held such a desire and hope that he would be normal. But this dissipated when even drug therapy wasn't sufficient to quiet his internal voices which, according to Carl, always broadcast a negative message.

He had so much happen to him—the death of his brother, becoming impotent due to the medication, and the fact he couldn't become the professional he wanted to be—that he was brought down, in spite of his artistic and creative talents and his natural ability to write descriptive poetry, which, in itself, could be therapeutic for his distressed mind.

Discrimination was everywhere

Torrey reminds us, "people diagnosed with schizophrenia will continue to be fourth-class citizens, leading twilight lives, shunned, ignored, neglected." He goes on to say, "nothing is going to change in the United States until an effective lobby begins to fight for the interest of those having schizophrenia."[10] Statistics indicate that research money allocated for the study of schizophrenia is only a fraction of what is spent to investigate heart disease. Why are more research dollars spent for a physical disease than for mental illness? In dealing with mental illness, there is discrimination at all levels: in areas of research as well as employment, medical care, finances, food and housing. With more than 220,000 members, The National Alliance for the Mentally Ill (NAMI) is the nation's leading grassroots advocacy organization dedicated solely to improving the lives of persons with severe mental illness.[11]

Rosalyn Carter, in her book, *Helping Someone With Mental Illness*, states that insurance companies limit inpatient treatment for mental health to only sixty days a year while there is no limit on the number of days of hospitalization for a physical ailment. In addition, the number of visits to a counselor is sharply limited when compared to unrestricted visits to other health care professionals. And the co-payment for mental illnesses is much higher than those for physical illnesses. This is a small example of the stigma being perpetuated by insurance companies."[12]

Our family experienced blatant discrimination when Steve and Carl died. Our insurance company refused to pay death benefits and burial expenses because their deaths were by suicide.

We experienced discrimination in treatment, also. Had Carl been admitted to the hospital for a brain tumor rather than a drug overdose due to a psychotic break, he would have been treated with respect. I observed the judgmental looks of the staff, and their abrupt and hasty attention to him. I felt their anger and impatience in treating someone who, to them, seemed so foolish and unthinking as to take an overdose. As I was walking into the room I overheard a nurse say, "Here's another kid trying to kill himself. I wonder what kind of home he comes from?" I felt intimidated by their accusations. It was if they were saying, "If you loved your child, this wouldn't have happened." Even in a so-called place of healing, the health care professionals' attitudes reflected intolerance as they ostracized, ignored, and feared our son. Their actions defied any understanding that mental illness is a chemical imbalance in the brain, not a choice made by our son.

Discrimination against mental illness is rampant in movies and television as well as in print media. People with mental illness are often called crazy, deranged, dangerous, or nuts. There was a movie produced, a comedy about suicide in which two college students are sure they can get straight A's if they can convince their roommate to commit suicide. Is this funny? I think not. I'm very offended when I see mental illness treated so glibly. A slogan I saw recently on a T-shirt reads, "I used to be schizophrenic but *we're* okay now." These messages reinforce the general public's perspective of understanding mental illness as something less than a "real" brain disease.

Ward and I experienced a waitress's insensitivity at a restaurant. After having had a lovely dinner with friends, we were introduced to each dessert. "The chocolate cake," she said, "is our suicide chocolate cake."

"Suicide cake?" I exclaimed. "What kind of name is that for a dessert?" I told her I was upset by the name of the cake, that after relaxing over a nice dinner, I didn't want to be brought back to my pain by hearing the word "suicide" used in such a glib manner. She walked away not understanding the impact on us.

In yet another restaurant a dessert was called, "Death by Suicide" cake. I appealed to the manager to change the name.

"There certainly must be a variety of adjectives that could describe a chocolate cake other than suicide," I said.

He apologized and sent us a gift certificate for a free dinner. The next time Ward and I dined there, I was pleased to note the "suicide cake" didn't appear on the menu. Friends have admitted that labeling a dessert "suicide" didn't bother them, but they expressed their gratitude to be made aware of those survivors whom it might offend. Attention to such details, minor to some but major to survivors of a loved one's suicide, heightens awareness for the general public.

Labeling

Another awareness issue surfaced for me. I became very sensitive to the stigma of labeling once Carl was diagnosed with schizophrenia. I overheard a person calling him "a mental case," and "a schizophrenic." Labeling Carl with a disease implies that he *is* the brain disorder. I, as well as others with loved ones with such disorders, would prefer to have them referred to as having a brain disorder or a psychiatric illness. This is the more compassionate way of seeing an individual as a special and unique human being.

A label indicates that the whole person in body, mind, and spirit is the illness when, in fact, the person is experiencing problems with the brain. Society tends to make the entire person the illness. In the medical community and in non-profit associations that support people with certain illnesses, the trend is to separate the person from the disease, such as saying, "This is a person with diabetes," rather than, "He is a diabetic." This identification should be extended to those with brain disorders as well. A person who has been diagnosed with a mental illness has a life apart from the disease. This individual might be a professional interior decorator or a parent of three children. Respect would be given the individual by focusing on his vast range of abilities rather than his disability in one area. As for referring to the "schizophrenic case," in my opinion this is the ultimate depersonalization of the person's individuality. If one is in treatment, he should be known and called by his name, not by a case label, number, or by his illness. This is another form of discrimination that needs to change.

As a parent of two children who suffered the ill effects of the disease, I admit that I look at discrimination and labeling from a personal perspective. However, I wish others would become aware that mental illness is no joke.

Even when I was a co-editor of a national music therapy journal some years ago, my colleague and I wrote a policy about respect of the individual. Contributors to the professional journal were required to respect the idea of labeling. We asked them to refer to the person first, then the disability, instead of using the disability as an adjective to describe the person. As the new language guidelines became clear, writers began expressing themselves differently.

This issue is my truth! I hope to be one of the voices that encourage the elimination of labeling and stereotypes that are thoughtless and uncaring. The President's Committee on Employment of People with Disabilities has published guidelines "to move our society to the point where disability status is only one variable in the full range of human experience."[13]

Labeling only perpetuates negative beliefs. I believe demonstrating compassion for others transmutes this energy of indifference into a positive form of expression. It is my hope that our new consciousness will transform public perception to reflect the same consideration for all people, regardless of mental or physical disabilities. As Ward and I became involved in the mental health system, we tried to learn about it and understand its workings.

The politics of mental health

E. Fuller Torrey, M.D. states, "the merging of mental illness and mental health early in the twentieth century has led to the politicalization of mental illness and to the diversion of its resources which have been major contributors to the mental illness crisis. He believes that society would be better served to separate mental illness from mental health and then to prioritize research and services so that the most severely ill go to the head of the line."[14]

Since Steve's and Carl's deaths, few changes have been made in mental health policy. Tipper Gore has been a strong voice for advances in mental health policy and she was quoted as saying, "I would hope that Congress would vote to strengthen loopholes in the Parity Law, to create laws that bring us into the 21st century, with equity where mental health illnesses are concerned and integrate it into health care in general."[15]

The Senate Committee on Health, Employment, Labor & Pensions (HELP) unanimously approved a parity bill, which was an important step forward to strengthen existing law and end discrimination in insurance coverage. It is unconscionable that this bill was defeated in December 2001. It would have covered the full range of mental illnesses and strengthened the 1996 law by prohibiting unequal limits on annual or lifetime mental health benefits, inpatient hospital days, outpatient visits, and out-of-pocket expenses.

Unfortunately, mental health services become lost in the political arena. It makes no sense that schizophrenia, manic-depressive illness, and other severe disorders are fair game for politics, whereas Parkinson's disease and Alzheimer's are not. The only way to dispel this myth, according to Torrey, is to "merge the brain disorders that we presently refer to as psychiatric illnesses with the brain disorders we call neurological illnesses. Thus schizophrenia, schizoaffective disorder, manic-depressive disorder, autism and severe forms of depression, panic disorder, and obsessive-compulsive disorder—the conditions defined as severe mental illnesses by the National Advisory Mental Health Council—could be merged with neurological illnesses such as multiple sclerosis, Parkinson's disease and Alzheimer's disease."[16]

When my husband and I were experiencing the injustice of the system, I felt pretty helpless. I did my part while our sons were involved in treatment, and I loved and supported my sons the best way I knew how. But there is just so much a parent can do. That's when I relied on support staff. But it is a lonely feeling. The professional staff let me know, in no uncertain terms, that they were equipped to help my sons more than we were. Part of me resisted that attitude because of my experience employed in a psychiatric hospital. Part of me was willing to let that happen. Who was I to believe, the staff or my sons? Sometimes I allowed myself to get sucked into my sons' version of the story, then I had to deal with the deep emotions I felt as I suffered along with the boys. It was hard to step back from this trauma that was going on in my life while the system perpetuated the myth that the illness could be cured.

I joined national mental health groups and advocated for legislation as a survivor of suicide. There is an old adage, "the squeaky wheel gets the grease." The wheels grind so slowly in the arena of mental illness. There needs to be more public concern and outrage.

Mental illness deserves a prioritization of our attention.

7

My Path Back From Tragedy

"Nothing can keep me from moving forward. Nothing."

Dr. David J. Walker[1]

My life journey

My life journey to healing the loss of my two sons has taken me on a long and painful path through the stages of grief. One thing I know: I would not have grown in these profound ways without these two horrendous losses in my life. I never would have believed that "time is a healer", but since the boys' deaths I have come to know myself more freely.

It was as if I had to recreate my life in a different way. Since the Spirit of Life is within everything and present at all times, my eyes have been opened by the death of my sons, so that I can see God's action in and around me. I moved beyond the stages of grief when I embraced the Light within, that all-powerful Spirit of Love. As I gave myself permission to be happy, my spiritual journey began. I know that a shift in my consciousness didn't happen through organized religion. It was only when I allowed myself to look within to find the cause of my fears that I woke up to an understanding of the power of Love. I became more focused on the beauty of life and strived to live in the moment. In leaving the past behind and not worrying about the future, I felt as if I was experiencing a spiritual awakening for the first time. For so long I had looked outside myself for mastery, only to discover that the wisdom I sought was within. I chose to embrace joy rather than spiral down into fear. I began to be aware of and identify every emotion that surfaced. Instead of ignoring the knot in my stomach or my throat's closing, I breathed in every negative feeling, acknowledged it, grieved over it, and embraced it. This painful but rewarding process took me from acceptance to transformation. Acknowledging this profound change of allowing and accepting the negativity as part of me, the Spirit of love has healed me.

Gerald Jampolsky, M.D., in his book, *Love is Letting Go Of Fear*, states there are only two emotions, fear and love.[2]

I acknowledge my fear of sadness.

I didn't acknowledge that my feelings of sadness were really feelings of fear. Somehow it seemed safer to say I was sad. In actuality I feared that sadness would overwhelm me, take over and plague me forever. To get in touch with that feeling, I went to the piano and played through my emotions until a feeling of love and peace came over me.

Music has always been an important part of my life. From the day I was born, I heard melodies of piano music floating through my soul. The image of my father sitting at the piano and improvising melodies inspired me to learn how to play. In the house where I grew up, our grand piano stood in the front room near the entrance of our house where my father's students would come and play day after day. I could sing the melodies that each student played. Soon I learned the same songs out of the same piano books sitting on the piano bench with my father at my side. So, my father had a huge influence on my love for music. Music feeds my soul.

Music was my great healer and consoler when our sons died. Daily I was drawn to my baby grand piano, the one I inherited from my dad. When I felt sad, depressed, and angry, I would play my soul creations. I felt some relief as I pounded on the piano and shouted out my rage at the boys for leaving me. Then, as if transfixed, my fingers naturally moved into something in a minor key, expressing my total despair and sadness. I missed them so much. As if some transforming power guided me, the slow, sad melodies I played would eventually lead into bright, flowing rhythms. I sang to Steve and Carl and had musical conversations with them. I sang about their births, their childhood, the fun and the heart-rending times we shared. As I expressed my innermost feelings, another mode or style of music would emerge. Each time I sat at the piano to "talk with the boys" my soul felt lighter, as if an enormous burden was being lifted. I knew the Spirit was guiding me; and, with each melody, pieces of my broken heart were being healed by allowing love to fill the void that once was filled with fear. Out of that release, I composed the words and lyrics to a song, "My Broken Heart," which expressed my journey from fear to peace. Just recently, that composition became my first single CD.

Music will always uplift me. I am in awe as I experience the power of music working wonders in my own and other people's lives. No wonder I became a music major in college, earned my master's degree in music therapy, worked in several clinical settings, and become a university professor of music therapy. I saw the importance of helping people with their emotional, physical, mental, and spiritual challenges by engaging them in the powerful tool of music.

I know how important it is to have found my sacred place of expression. While I communicate through music, others may find they are taken to places beyond themselves through their gardening or painting. It doesn't matter what it is as long as we each find fulfillment and happiness by listening to our hearts and doing what our hearts tells us to do. My heart transmuted my fear of sadness. Music gave me some answers.

I identified my fear of what people think of me.

Ward and I were invited to be guest speakers at a bereavement group, an alliance for parents of children who have died. Thinking this would be the perfect opportunity to speak about our feelings of alienation and separation in a safe environment, we happily accepted the invitation. However, as I listened to the sad stories from grieving parents and eventually told mine, I discerned a subtle message. Whereas their children had died by accident, my children had intentionally taken their own lives. Thinking I was with people who would understand my feelings, instead I felt only judgment, blame, and shame directed toward me and our family. I left that meeting angry and upset. I realized that some of the anger I felt was carried over from my childhood need to please others and my need for approval. I was afraid of what they thought of me. That night I broke my tennis racket while hitting my bed and the floor in a flurry of anger. The experience not only cost me my tennis racket, but brought home to me that I had to find a better way to vent my frustration. Also, it was very clear to me that our ministry was to be with people who knew the anguish of suicide.

I acknowledged my fear of death.

Following my sons' suicides, I feared that Marcia and Kathy, and even Ward, would die. Though I realized these thoughts were irrational, they plagued me nonetheless.

I needed to know where our sons went after making their transition to the other side. I believe there is no death, and that our eternal soul lives on after the physical body dies, but I wanted to know *where* it lives. After posing this question, I had many experiences to help me understand.

A week after Steve died, I contacted a medium to see if Steve could be reached. This is a person who connects with forces beyond the physical world into the afterlife. I was very nervous about this consultation. The medium told me that a helper, named Eno, was assigned to Steve, and that Eno wanted to speak to me.

I listened as he spoke.

"Steve can't talk to you right now because he's resting, but I have a message for you from him. He says that he didn't mean to take his own life, and that he was very surprised to find himself here on the other side." I was totally surprised at this message, but I have to admit that hearing that Steve didn't really want to leave us was somehow comforting.

After both Steve and Carl died, I dreamed of them. They appeared together, wearing gray jogging suits. They were both smiling from ear to ear, and they had their arms around each other, laughing and dancing. They looked at me; and, although they didn't speak, I sensed they were telling me they were okay and not to worry. The next morning I told Ward about my dream. Surprisingly, he shared that he had had the same dream the night before but he hadn't mentioned it because he was afraid my feelings would be hurt. So it was our mutual feeling and joy that our boys were definitely "alive" on the other side and were eager to communicate with us.

I believe our sons contacted us in other ways, too. The first Christmas after Carl's death, I walked into the living room just as my favorite music box began playing without having been wound. It played once, then stopped. I knew in my mother's heart that Carl was letting me know he was there with me.

Another revelation came to me through a psychic a couple of years after Steve died. Marcia called excitedly saying, "Mom, I just talked with my friend, Rita, and she has a message for you from Steve.

"What did she say," I asked eagerly.

Steve says, 'I forgive you.' Rita assured me you would know what that means," said Marcia.

"Yes, dear, I know exactly what that means. Thank you, and thank Rita for me." I was so happy. This was a conclusion to one of the unresolved conversations I'd had with Steve. He, in his perfect love, had forgiven me for controlling him, and I knew he had also forgiven himself.

Years later, when our daughters and their families came to visit for the Christmas holidays, Ward reached in his office closet to retrieve a game.

A picture of our four children fell swirling to the floor. The colored photo brought back sweet memories of our children as teenagers, all smiling broadly, sitting on Santa's lap. I knew it was a wonderful message from our boys that they wanted to join in our family celebration. We all looked at the picture with fond memories, then I put it on our refrigerator door where it remains today along with all our other family pictures.

Multiple experiences have convinced me that our loved ones contact us in our sleeping state. One week after my mother made her transition, she appeared to me in a dream. I felt a great, tangible warmth as she kissed me and told me she loved me.

Carl, Steve, Kathy, and Marcia, Christmas celebration, 1979.

I remember thinking, *I'm so happy because now we can begin building a good relationship with each other*. When I woke up, I was elated to have learned that, although we hadn't connected very well in this lifetime, she would always love me.

These personal experiences demonstrated to me that there is no death, only a transition from our third dimensional world of duality to another dimension of being.

But this prompted other questions. If I believe that death is not the end, then in what form does the soul live on? I read that many faiths believe the soul continues beyond the physical form, that the very nature of the soul is unity and oneness with the Source, All That Is.

When Ward and I discussed this subject, he had this to say: "I believe we are made of God's thoughts and God's Light, which death can't destroy. I think humans are a hologram of thoughts and God's consciousness which physical death can't destroy. If death were the end, then God ceases to exist."

Another question I had concerning our sons' dying at such a young age was about life path. Is the life path for each person preordained? How much choice do we have? Some believe we have a 25% chance to choose our destiny, with the other 75% being decided for us. Others suggest the ratio is 50-50. Still others contend we have no free will at all, that we don't make any choices, that consciousness is all there is. I believe we each have a master plan, a blueprint, a DNA if you will, that allows us our choices as well as dictates our boundaries. I resonate to the idea that our souls make the decision as to our next mission on earth.

I have paraphrased these thoughts from Neale Donald Walsch's book, *Friendship With God*.

> It is my will that all that has occurred in my life should occur. All incidents of my life have led me to this moment. I was given the perfect mother and the perfect father to prepare me for this assignment I have given myself; the perfect family situation and the perfect childhood. Nothing has happened to me by accident, nothing has occurred by chance. It has been called forth, all of it that I may experience and know what I choose to experience.[3]

I accept that our children chose us as their parents for their lessons as well as ours. I believe that Steve, at age twenty-seven, and Carl, at age thirty, fulfilled their divine plan on this earth plane and chose to leave. As a result of their passing, which felt early to us, Ward and I began our search for an understanding of death and of the life beyond existence on this mortal plane. My heart transmuted my fear of death. My spirit gave me some answers.

I acknowledged my fear of abandonment.

While in Oklahoma in 1996, Ward had a near death experience (NDE). I feared he would leave me. It was what some describe as a typical NDE experience, though at the time we had no background in the phenomenon. Previous to this he had been sick with flu-like symptoms for three days and was dehydrated. As he became weaker, we wondered if he might have food poisoning, recalling the last evening meal when I had eaten something different.

In his Near Death Experience, Ward saw a beautiful light. Slowly he floated above his body and then looked down to see himself lying on a slab. Three men dressed in robes came to him and told him he was to work with "the Angel of Death" to help people who were terminally ill. The light was so comforting and loving that Ward didn't want to come back, but the men insisted his work on earth wasn't done. They told him he had lost his joy and needed to recapture it. Reluctantly, Ward came back into his physical body, depleted from the experience. Energy workers used Reiki [4] for several hours, a healing system that involves the laying on of hands and healing touch, to help him regain the energy drained from his NDE experience.

When Ward told me about the beautiful light that surrounded him and that he didn't want to come back, I lost it and yelled at him.

"What do you mean, you didn't want to come back? I have lost two sons, and I'm not ready to lose you," I cried.

I was beside myself, feeling such fear about his leaving me. I finally calmed down. I listened to his intense experience, and we wept together, affirming our love for each other.

Out of that profound experience Ward wrote his dissertation on Death and Dying. With his firsthand experience and a greater understanding of existence on the other side, he lost his fear of death. I know I can't find happiness or connect with the Light within through anyone else's assurance, but I was touched by his experience. My heart transmuted my fear of abandonment. My soul mate helped me find some answers.

> I acknowledged my fear of taking risks
> that would sever my sense of connection to community.

I was affected by Ward's experience, but knew I had to go through a deeper dark night of my soul to understand the impact of risk taking.

While in Oklahoma, Ward and I both felt a need to disengage from our formal roles in the spiritual community. In doing so, once again our life fell apart. Without employment and with time on our hands, we had no choice but to look within. In my solitude I felt restless and once again came face to face with my demons. I was angry with this new situation. I didn't think it was fair that I needed to quit my job as director of music for the church just because Ward had quit his. But under the circumstances, I felt that was my best choice. Typical of my ways of coping, I sought answers through external wisdom and took a class on the Inner Child, hoping to find answers. In grace, this time an experience did, in fact, open a new pathway of self discovery that not only temporarily deepened my pain, but ultimately led to what would become my transformation.

After several sessions of a class on the Inner Child and becoming involved in various classroom activities, I found myself a ready volunteer when the facilitator posed the following question: "Who would like to be rocked?"

An overwhelming stirring swelled deep within me, letting me know in an instant the gentle act of a mother's loving embrace was an aching need within. A friend gently took me in her arms; and, in her tender rocking motion, at age fifty-nine, I felt a release from the pain of abandonment and a deepening of my capacity to give and receive love. I was filled with a new sense of joy knowing I had the courage and strength to ask for help. I discovered the key to receiving is asking and being open to the message. My heart transmuted my fear of taking risks. My open heart helped me find the answers.

> I acknowledged my fear of losing control.

As a child, I felt my parents viewed me as rebellious and outrageous. They lived by the rules, and I didn't want to be put in a box. They repressed their feelings, and I wanted to express mine openly. They wanted everything and everyone to be perfect, and I wanted to know the truth. We were on different wavelengths. The message instilled in me and driven home repeatedly was, "Think before you act so people won't think badly of us," which I interpreted to mean, "I should be proper." Of course, it wasn't conscious on their part. Nevertheless, at a very young age, I learned it wasn't safe to trust my feelings. It felt as if they robbed me of who I truly was, a beautiful child whose essence was pure sweetness. I felt everything deeply in my heart, including love, compassion, anger, and fear and longed to express these feelings passionately. Yet my parents said I couldn't act that way. I was genuinely hurt. The outcome was that I blamed myself for all the losses in my life. If others suffered, it was my fault.

A wise friend advised that I needed to reclaim myself. In order to break through my adapted mental state, he said, I needed to free up the feelings I held in my physical body. He warned this might involve having to do things I would find uncomfortable.

In a beautiful setting overlooking the Pacific Ocean, Ward and I sat at a lovely luncheon table where five of us gathered. As I sat there enjoying the fellowship of friends, an idea flashed before me. *Could this setting be an opportunity for me to experiment with being uncomfortable?*

Gathering courage, tears welled up in my eyes as I heard old parent tapes telling me this would be very improper. However, I was determined to pull this off regardless of those inner tapes. I waited until everyone had cleared their plates. There was a pause in the conversation. With my fingers, I picked up the remaining fettuccini noodles strewn on my plate and began shoving them in my mouth. As I chewed noisily I talked loudly about a movie I liked. Stunned but accepting, Ward and my friends watched as I devoured the last bite. Then I excused myself to wash the specks of food off my glasses. While I was in the bathroom, I heard those parent tapes once more—my mother, in this case—telling me she was horrified.

I was able to laugh and say, "It's okay, Mother. I'm just learning how to be me." My friends laughed with me and affirmed my courage to "act improperly." I felt free of some baggage I had been carrying around for a long time. I forgave myself. My heart transmuted my fear of losing control. By exerting my courage, I reclaimed my personal power.

I identified my fear of intimacy.

Soon after Steve died, I was quilting with a dear friend from our church congregation. She looked up at me and said, "Tell me about Steve, Mary. I would love to know more about him."

My grief was so new and my emotions so raw I kept our conversation at a superficial level, knowing I couldn't talk about Steve without breaking into tears. I know she would have cried with me, but I kept up my guard and refused to let her in.

My excuse for not sharing my *real* feelings was not trusting her to keep confidential the intimate details of my life lest it become gossip in the church. I pushed her away, not allowing intimacy.

I was the loser. I missed receiving the blessing of another's ministering to me. It was as if I put a filter on what was coming to me so I received only what I thought I could handle. I felt profound regret as I realized how many opportunities I had missed, as well as the rejection others must have felt by my inability to receive their love.

Recently, I had an opportunity to open my heart and share my innermost fears with a friend while writing this book. As I expressed the shame I felt at my sons' taking their own lives, I began to cry. Much to my surprise my friend began crying also, and we held each other and sobbed. In this moment I felt love energy tingle throughout my body and a pulsing I had never felt before. My acceptance of this great gift of intimacy changed my fear.

I revisited my fear of intimacy.

I discovered my fear of intimacy was connected to victimhood. Until I dealt with that fear, it would recur again and again. After Steve died, I continued church responsibilities with a smile on my face. I sang in the adult choir, directed the children's choir, and played in the hand bell choir. At rehearsals, no one spoke Steve's name. Since I was afraid to express my feelings, others were hesitant to bring up the subject of Steve's death. This silence created an uncomfortable impasse among members of the congregation and me. I rationalized that, had I been willing to express my grief, no one would have heard my pain anyway because of my role in the church. Ward was hired as their pastor, and that leadership role put us on a pedestal that perpetuated the myth that we couldn't be reached. I shut out my heart's desire to share my innermost feelings because of my fears.

To work through this fear I recently shared my fragile feelings with a group of friends. I bravely talked about a subject I had avoided for many years: Steve's and Carl's taking street drugs. To my relief they were very accepting of me and didn't make any judgments about my experiences.

When they asked questions about the boys' involvement with the drugs and the possible connection to inducing schizophrenia, I stayed centered, answered questions, and didn't take their comments personally. As a result I bonded with several of the women. Talking about these personal issues helped me dispel my fears. Acknowledging my sense of victim-hood helped me work through the fear of intimacy.

I identified another issue of intimacy.

Recently I made a treasure map.[5] Treasure mapping engages the active use of imagination with the help of visual aids which enables a person to visualize and enhance the quality of their imagination. It expresses a person's inner desires. I was told to let my higher self, not my mind, choose the pictures and words and paste them onto to a poster board. The higher self knows what we need. By mapping my treasure visually, I am impressing the image of the treasure repeatedly into my consciousness. When the idea is received into my consciousness, the treasure manifests itself in some unique manner. I was skeptical but agreed to try this. My focus was to express my desire for my book to be published. I chose a bright yellow poster board and set out the scissors, glue and a pile of magazines. I began tearing out photographs of flowers, the ocean, dolphins, as well as "sayings" to which I was immediately drawn. I kept seeing pictures of dogs, but I resisted cutting them out. *The only reason I would have dogs on my treasure map,* I rationalized, *would be because of Carl's love for dogs.* I finally chose a small picture of a cocker spaniel and pasted it in the upper right corner of my treasure map underneath a picture of two boys who represented Steve and Carl. Even then the thought of that dog kept nagging at me.

In a meditation several weeks later I knew why. I began seeing visions of the dogs we'd had during our marriage. There was Auggie, a white fuzzy little peek-a-poo; Ginger, a spunky cocker spaniel; Boris, a coal-black puppy; Laskey, a German shepherd mix who had a litter of six puppies; and last, but not least, Jonah, a miniature Doberman. As I saw each dog, I pondered what my relationship was to them. Did I train them? Did I take care of them? Did I love them? I discovered that, except for Auggie, Ward and the children paid more attention to them than I did. In fact, the feeling that came over me was that I only tolerated the dogs and, in the case of Jonah, pushed him away when he came over to snuggle at my feet while I was quilting.

I had pushed the dogs away from me. *Why, what is my fear?* I asked myself. Then I suddenly had a great insight. I was pushing love away. *If I pushed the dogs' love away,* I thought, *who else have I done that to?* I knew in my heart of hearts I had done that in some of my relationships too. So I had to look at my intimacy issues and my fears around them.

One of the many ways I pushed intimacy away was to control the conversation. I felt it appropriate for me to ask the other person questions about his personal life; but, if I was asked something personal, I'd find a way to divert the subject. I would focus on the other person, so he would not get too close to who I really was.

So why do I do this? I pondered. Fear, fear, fear, fear! I realized my energy field, as a young child, had been violated with verbal abuse and disempowering attitudes. I wasn't encouraged to be independent and thrive outside the control of my parents, and thus I had been stripped of the personal power I needed for health and success. I uncovered an old, very powerful attitude. I found a new freedom knowing the root of my inner fear. In daily meditation, a practice I adopted when I was in Hawaii, I asked for divine guidance for this attitude to be transformed. When I did, I was immediately engulfed in a feeling of love. Again, my heart transmuted my fear of intimacy. Meditation helped me find the answers.

> And finally, I understand the complexity of my journey.
> I acknowledge that I need to revisit my fears
> and come face to face with my resistance to total surrender.

Of the two dominant emotions, fear and love, I choose *love.* I've learned not to judge what I think and place no blame on myself or anyone else. There is neither right nor wrong. I experience a big shift when I don't resist my fears. In the past I resisted love, now I find it's easier and more enjoyable allowing people into my life. Everything is about being aware of my feelings and honoring what I think. It's about living in the moment, embracing love and having no attachments, judgments, or expectations. My daily goal is to love myself and others with no strings attached.

It seems that on my journey I am given help when I need it most. To help Ward and me with our healing, a very intuitive woman shared this story with our friend. She said, "I see this couple (Ward and me) as Light workers who were given these two sons in this lifetime to work with and guide because of the boys' unique needs. Their short time here with them

moved them further along 'on the chessboard' so to speak. Tell this couple that it's not a question of what they did wrong in rearing their sons,
but rather a question of what they did right. God gave them these two
special souls to teach; they did what they were supposed to do, and now
the boys have gone on their way back to the Infinite, to await their next
incarnation. They are all the better for having been here."

My morning ritual includes lighting a candle and listening to my
heart. As I sit quietly, I feel a warmth in my heart as I enjoy the feeling of
a very deep and profound silence. This is, for me, awareness of the Light
within. In this silence, I am calmed, inspired, and changed. I ask questions and receive insights into what my soul wants for me that day.

My journey has been long, but rewarding. My search in remembering
who I am is getting clearer. I have shifted from believing in an external
Source, whom I blamed for all that happened, to the understanding that
the Source is within me. Paramahansa Yogananda said: "When you feel
your consciousness in every atom, in all space, and beyond creation, then
you can rightfully say, God and I are one."[6] This truth makes me responsible for everything that happens to me. And it also makes Steve and Carl
responsible for everything that happened to them. The Light in me and
the Light in them are One. Knowing this has helped me comprehend
that the Light within places me as a co-creator of my life experiences,
freeing me to be myself, to be responsible for myself, and giving me joy to
celebrate that I am a Light worker.

I have embarked on a journey that has taken me through the pain of
each stage of grief and beyond the final stage of acceptance to make my
passage one of Spirit. The complex and often haphazard way my fears
have surfaced have caused me to go deeper through the dense layers of repressed feelings. My intent to see the Light and find peace has not been
without resistance, yet I remain committed to total surrender. Along the
way, I have recovered my joy and noticed changes in myself as a result of
my intention to live in the Light.

I have decided that being proper and having common sense are no fun
anymore. They aren't of Spirit anyway. I choose to be spontaneous and
outrageous again. I have reclaimed who I am. I live in the moment rather
than holding on to what happened yesterday or worrying what will happen tomorrow. No one speaks for me. I speak my truth as I know it. My
self-worth has improved. I used to give my power away to others. Now
when I feel myself re-living that pattern, I ask for divine guidance to help

me do what is best for my highest good. I'm in touch with my feelings and express them more honestly. I'm aware of my patterns of denial and take responsibility for my feelings and actions. Whenever I have a problem, I know it comes from my belief in limiting thought patterns that take me back into pain and suffering. I solve my problems by being more positive. Because I have opened up, communication has improved between Ward and me. Instead of "stuffing" my anger, I express my feelings when I'm upset. In knowing who I am, I am able to establish healthy boundaries in my relationships. In forgiving myself, I love myself. Instead of being so serious, I can laugh at myself.

All the growth and healing does not, however, negate a mother's pain. I echo Iris Bolton's sentiment through her words and mine as a way of describing a mother's pain.[7] I finally gave myself permission to be angry at my sons for giving up, for leaving me with such pain, for leaving my life, for not allowing me or others to help them, for their choice about their lives, and for our lost futures together. As I worked through that anger, that destructive power that had disempowered me for so long was resolved.

I thought for a long time that my goal should be to grow to a place of total letting go of the boys so my pain would be gone. I have faced my fears and opened up to support from my soul mate, daughters, extended family and friends. I have embraced spiritual growth as a path to transformation. And instead of coming to a place of surrender that releases all of my pain, experiences, connections, and memories of them, I honor the pain that represents my love for them. Surrendering has meant knowing my personal connection to a Higher Power and knowing that power exists within all things. When I hold the vision of what I want to see happen, I reclaim my power and know I'm a co-creator of love in this universe.

This became clear to me as I examined my resistance to visit the final resting place of my two sons. Like others who face the untimely death of a loved one, we struggled at the time with final arrangements for Steve and Carl. Our decision on the inscriptions for their tombstone was excruciating, helped only by our desire to portray who they had been while on this earth plane.

In tribute to Steven and Carl whose remains are together in Grand Rapids, Michigan their tombstone reads:

Steven Ward Scovel. Born: May 31, 1961. Died: June 23, 1988. He was a musician. (Etched into his side of the tombstone is a musical staff and notes.)

Carl John Scovel. Born: May 10, 1963. Died: June 18, 1993. He was an artist. (On his side of the tombstone is an etching of an artist's palette.)

8

Letters of love

As music and art were powerful healing tools for my family and me, another equally effective healing process is writing. Writing a personal essay, poem, or letter enables the writer to express deep feelings about whatever needs attention.

When a loved one takes his own life it leaves its scars on all family members. In the letters that follow Ward, Marcia, Kathy, and I have written about our heart experiences with Steve and Carl. Ward shares how much he misses his sons and reiterates what a great spiritual gift he has received from them, while Marcia and Kathy poignantly express their feelings and memories of their brothers. They share brief stories of happy memories with Steven and Carl and describe their dismay at the choice their brothers made. Not only did the deaths leave a void in their lives, their brothers' suicides also meant that their children would never know their uncles' love.

A tribute to my brothers from Marcia, a loving sister

I had never heard my dad cry before. So when dad and mom called, both crying, to tell me Steve had killed himself, it added to the sadness and reality of it all. The first thing that came out was "Why?" Why would he kill himself when he had such a loving and understanding family? Didn't he know we would've done anything to help him? Didn't he know we were worried about him? Didn't he know we cared? What state would he have to be in to kill himself, to feel so helpless that he couldn't approach his loving, supportive family?

I remember Steve as a happy all-American kid with a smile always on his face. He loved music so much; it was such an integral part of him. Steve was music! He was always singing in his head, tapping his fingers to a beat only he heard. He was happiest when he was playing trumpet, piano, in musicals and plays. I remember when he was the boy in "Amahl and the Night Visitors." He practiced hobbling around with that stick for weeks. He was so cute with his high voice and glasses singing right out to the audience. When he was older, he and Carl started a sing-o-gram business. These musical times were the essence of Steve! But he was always doing fun things. In Ohio he rode his unicycle ten miles into the nearest town. He got a ride back home and when I asked him if it hurt, he said, "Yea, I was a little sore, but it was fun." For the job he had at an ice cream shop, he rode an old fashioned bike with the large wheel in front and small one in back that he had to run and jump to get on.

All those fun times represented who Steve was. So sometimes I feel sad because he was so gifted and talented, and he didn't get to fulfill himself in his goals and ideals. I feel sad at his choices and that he couldn't confide in us. I also feel sad that after being homeless in New York City he seemed to have lost his spirit and became blank inside. There was a time in Michigan, after he had returned from NYC, that he was asked to play the guitar for a group. He said "yes," but this time he was unable to find the chords on the guitar or carry the tune and they pulled the plug on him. I feel sad when I remember that.

Steve did call me collect once from California. He said he had been thinking about what had happened in NYC. "What did happen in NYC?" I asked. He said he had gone there to find someone to produce his music and a producer promised to help him in return for Steve sleeping with him. He was upset that the guy never followed through on his promise. So I asked him what he was doing in California and he said living on the beaches waiting to contact producers. I asked how he was going to make contacts living on the beaches, and why doesn't he come home? Well, that shut him down and he said he was going to go, so I backed off because I didn't want him to hang up. I talked about what was going on with me and told him I missed him and loved him. He said he loved me too. I told him he could always call and talk, but I never heard from him again.

I have different feelings with each of my brothers' deaths. With Steve, I dealt with the "whys," the shock that he killed himself and that I didn't know he was under that much mental anguish. I wished he had left a letter explaining why. Steve endured his pain by himself. Several months after he died I went through a divorce. For about ten years after these two events occurred, I was still unable to remember the year they happened. With Carl, he was always telling immediate family how lonely and bored he was, often talked about suicide and attempted it several times. I was around Carl during some of these tough times and Carl's death felt like a loss.

When I think of Carl, I smile and remember his sense of humor. He was always the one to put rabbit ears behind someone's head during a picture, eat a bag of oranges before anyone else even had one, or make sure you opened his present first. He coined our family's expression "TB," pronounced, "TeeeBeeee," and short for "Too Bad." This was an expression to be used any time for anyone, especially when you didn't really mean it. For example, if you were outvoted in your choice of movie to watch, someone could say, "TeeeBeeee." Yea, that was Carl: get with reality! He was also good at bringing levity into a situation that was getting too serious. I remember once when I was getting wound up about something, he went into this rap talk and movement and said, "Hey, Marcia, man, you too heavy man." Well that changed the tone! Carl had another phrase that described his basic philosophy, and it was "Smooth, loose and cool." I think he created this when he was writing poems and it had something to do with rock and roll. Carl wrote a lot of poems. They usually started out with a great inspirational theme on love or friendship, then got sidetracked to something else, leaving you scratching your head wondering just what the message was. But he was always so proud and intense about them I just "oohed" and "ahhed" at the parts that were clear. There was one poem called "Fanagel the Bagel," that he wrote music for and turned into a song. It was a pretty funny song and he contacted bagel places to see if they would use it for advertising. Although he never heard from any bagel businesses it was a hit at our house!

The hardest part for me was when Carl would call, depressed and talking about killing himself. Many times I wished I hadn't answered the phone. I would rack my brain for my crisis phone training from college and reflect that part of him must not want to die if he was calling me. After saying that a few times, he would just say, "Yea, yea." He was not a person into denial! He felt his loneliness, spoke his depression, and expressed his unhappiness. He didn't like being lonely and not having a girlfriend. During these times he would just say, "this sucks." We would then talk about life, I might give advice, tell him what I was doing. He would always say good-bye by thanking me for talking and saying he loved me. I was always grateful I had talked with him.

If I had a chance to say something to my brothers I would say that I love you both. I'm glad we were a fun and close family and I have a lot of smiling memories. I tell my daughters stories about you, I still cry, and I live with your spirits, which were both so full of love. I send my brothers love.

A tribute to my brothers from Kathy, a loving sister

I went into shock when I received the phone call at work that Steve had killed himself. My mind ceased to function, and I went on "auto-pilot." A part of me could not accept this new reality, so gratefully my brain shut down and went into "survival mode." "Call my husband, Richard—yes, I can do that. Meet him somewhere, somewhere—I could not grab onto any concrete information—yes, the Post Office—I know where that is!"

You never know what life has in store for you, what ups and downs will become a part of your path. Right after Steve died, I was forced to re-evaluate my beliefs. Is it possible to rear a child in the best, most loving environment and still not make a difference in how that person turns out? Have we no control at all?

Over the years I've come to realize that the minute I try to structure my life a certain way, "Divine Mother" will have another plan. I need to repeatedly let go of having my way so that God can have her say in my life. I've come to see that we may not be able to control our circumstances, but we always have a choice in how we deal with each situation. Having a positive attitude and knowing that I can still have a deep inner joy, no matter what happens, is my salvation. I cannot rely on outer circumstances for my happiness.

Death made me extremely grateful for life. I realized how precious it was. I vowed not to take anyone or anything for granted. I wanted to live every moment to its fullest—banish all fears and get on with life. Not waste a moment. How often do we deeply understand the preciousness of life? This truly was a gift from my brothers.

I never blamed God. How could I? I knew both brothers were brave warriors who each in turn fought their own great battle. I knew Steve and Carl were with God and in a much better space than here on Earth. I knew they were finally at peace. This knowledge comforted me, especially when I thought of Carl, who had tried for so long to be happy and live a normal, fulfilling life. The stamina and perseverance that he had has been an inspiration to me. He had incredible willpower to overcome adversity, to move on, and to try yet again.

When I think of them now, my thoughts are occasionally laced with regret that they are not here to share an experience, or to see their nephew grow up. My son never knew his uncles, and that makes me very sad. However, I often think of them and I get a grin on my face as I recall the fun times we had together, or something they said or did.

Today I still miss Steve and Carl and wish they were here, but I can also thank them for the precious gift they gave me-a chance to delve deeper into myself and find happiness that is not dependent on outer circumstances.

I send Steve and Carl love and light.

A letter from a loving father

Dear Steve and Carl,

As I begin writing this letter to you, I start feeling both my grief and my love for you over and over again. I feel the pain in my heart and stomach and I don't breathe in a normal way. I hurt because you're not with me in the physical so I can hug and kiss you and hear what you are thinking and saying.

I want you to know that because of your deaths, I have changed in ways I think are good. I look at your transition as a great and wonderful gift to me. I now know, that in an esoteric and metaphysical sense, you didn't die, you just changed your consciousness. Your souls never die, they grow in wisdom and live on forever. Another piece of the gift for me is that I know I'm not separate from you and God. We are all one in love and in the Spirit. I now experience joy in living, as my fear and the fear of death is gone. I am free to love you and others with complete trust, that wherever love will lead me, I am open to the moment of being vulnerable and true to myself.

You boys have given me this, the greatest gift of all, a knowing to accept whatever comes to me in life, even your deaths, as a spiritual gift. It is to live in a state of peace, love and non-resistance, for I can live in this world and not be afraid of the pain and suffering and death that is here. It is all an illusion. Our real life is in the Spirit. Another gift you gave me, after your deaths, is the realization that nothing is outside of myself. God is within and so is my dark side and I embrace all of what I am, so the divine purpose of the universe is able to unfold through me. This is why we human beings are so important to the spiritual purpose of the universe.

Your mother, sisters, nieces and nephew, and myself are very close and share our lives and love with each other; however, we haven't forgotten your love for us and how we laughed and cried with each other through the early years. But I know, it is "in the moment" that we continue to touch each other and the Spirit of the loving God.

I still cry when I read your mother's book as her loving words bring me back to those moments of grief and death and not being in your physical presence. I feel much better as time goes on, but I will always miss you and miss hugging and kissing you, my dear sons.

Your loving Dad

Letters from a loving mother

Dear Steve,

I miss you so much. In your brief time on earth, Steve, you brought me much joy. We had such a special relationship and I miss your hugs, your sweet, sensitive spirit and your tender way of saying, "Hi, Mom." I loved your incredible enthusiasm for life, your beautiful tenor voice, your bouncing energy while playing trumpet in the marching band, your smile of pride and sheer joy while balancing on the unicycle, and the cute way you brushed back your thick and wavy hair.

I smile, fondly remembering the numerous times we spent down on the floor, on our hands and knees, frantically looking for your contact lens, watching you diligently brush your teeth as you strolled through the house, and adoring you as you swerved in and out of the water on the slalom ski. I will always hold you in my heart my beloved son.

No matter how harsh the past events were, I will always remember our happy and loving times together. Thank you, Steve, for being my son and bringing me your gift of love.

Your loving Mom

Dear Carl,

Carl, I miss you and your wonderful smile. I miss your love. I have such fond memories of you when you were four years old, playing the violin in a group of twelve other children. You knew exactly where to place your tiny fingers on the strings of the violin to make music flow from your instrument. I loved it when you willingly used your artistic talents to draw something I needed for one of my classes. I was in awe of the ease with which you created your art. You observed everything I did. You always noticed when I had a new hairdo or if I needed more curls. When we lived on a farm for three years, I always knew I could find you in the barn with the animals. You so loved your "critters." I dearly loved to see you interacting with your niece Kayla and nephew Dylan. Your eyes danced as you held them in your arms and played with them. I always enjoyed our discussions about spirituality. When we discovered you had schizophrenia, I remember the strange outfits you would wear. I never knew what you would look like when your dad and I would pick you up. I loved you deeply, Carl, just for who you were, my warm, sensitive, and loving young man. Thank you, Carl, for bringing such love to my heart.

Your loving Mom

The pain in my heart that represents enduring love for Steve and Carl rests within the Light and love that my spiritual journey has helped me discover. I know my journey will continue as I dig deeper through the levels of fear and open more fully to the grace of the Light within. For it is that Light that helps me endure my pain and accept myself.

One day while driving home, I was singing along to the music of the Messiah. Suddenly I was prompted to turn off the tape player and sing one of my favorite songs, The Rose. [8] After I sang the words, "It's the heart afraid of breaking that never learns to dance," I abruptly stopped singing. I had tears in my eyes. Spirit spoke to me, "Mary, by embracing your broken heart you have learned to dance." And I joyfully knew, "Yes, my heart is still broken, and I love my broken heart."

9

Healing The Inner Self

"Let choice whisper in your ear and love murmur
in your heart. Here comes *Life.*"[1]

Maya Angelou

Though at the time I felt the pain of the loss of my beloved sons, I did not have the information I would later uncover through my journey to the Light within. At that point, not only did I not love my broken heart, I was, in fact, not interested in connecting to my heart at all; the pain too much to bear. But Steve and Carl came into my life as my teachers. They gave me the gift of love, and it is through these new eyes that I can see love's great light.

Now I want to share the light and love with you, for anything less than that would not honor their essence or mine.

Perhaps you have pain in your life as a survivor of the suicide of a loved one or an attempt yourself; perhaps you are a health-care provider, educator, or friend in witness of the pain in another; or perhaps you have undergone a different kind of personal pain that seems too much in the moment to endure. Think now for a moment about getting in touch with your pain. Are you willing to put aside denial and go into the present moment knowing you will survive? Are you willing to begin your journey to your Light within?

This journey that you will undertake will fully engage your mind, body, and spirit as you discover the Light within. By mind, I mean knowledge, understanding, and thinking that goes beyond the daily chatter of your self-talk, that constant stream of tapes you play that keep you rooted in the past. By body, I mean the physical nature of our existence including our external and internal connections, being in touch with the feelings and cues within your body and within your external world. By spirit, I mean the ways in which you know there is something beyond yourselves, whatever your beliefs, religious practice or persuasion, the acknowledgment of God, a Higher Power or a Source that lies outside the human limitations.

The following open-ended prompts evolved from my own personal journey and are designed to lead you to discover the Light within. As part of your journey, expect that you will travel through the stages of grief, for these cannot be omitted. (See Appendix B)

My experience has been for those stages of grief to overlap and come back at different levels of intensity to be resolved again and again as I dug deeper into myself. In order to see the gifts that this loss would give, I had to go beyond these stages to uncover fully the truth of my pain. Making the body, mind, spirit connection helped me find the peace of the Light within because in the Light there is no limitation. These prompts helped me do that. And now I encourage you, as well, to take this last leg of your journey by quietly reflecting on each prompt.

Quiet your mind in the stillness to reflect.
Tune into your body and attend to your physical impulses.
Open your heart to the still, small voice of spirit.

My greatest heart's desire is   _____

I am vulnerable when   _____

My deepest secret is   _____

My deepest pain is   _____

My deepest failures (real or imagined) are _____

My deepest fears are   _____

I engage with the world around me by _____

Music transforms me when   _____

My connection with nature helps me to know _____

The color, texture & tone of my immediate environment reveal ____

Ways in which I listen to my body are _____

Experiences where I know I am not alone are _____

If I created a picture right now, it would be _____

I eliminate chaos in my life when I _____

I find comfort in my living space when I _____

Ways in which I create loving relationships with all living things include _____

As I strive to reclaim who I am, I acknowledge my mistakes such as _____

Ways in which I am true to myself, even if it means disappointing others, are _____

Ways in which I practice self-love are _____

Ways in which I can stay "in the moment" are _____
Way in which I can practice unconditional love for myself
and others are _____
Ways in which I see joy, beauty and opportunities in my world
instead of challenges, test and negativity are _____
Ways in which I can practice not resisting are _____
Ways in which I can practice not taking things personally are _____
Ways in which I can practice forgiveness, that is, seeing a person's
innocence are _____
Ways in which I can give up judging myself and others are _____
Ways I can release resentments are _____
Accepting the truth that whatever I ask for is already mine
frees me to _____
Practicing going into meditation, to be alone with myself,
turning inward so Spirit can speak to me and through me,
will change and inspire me to _____
Accepting the truth that I am Divine Love frees me to _____

As you step into the flow of Spirit, be aware of all the gifts that can come
to you. Open your heart to the possibilities that through devastating pain
you can feel love, freedom, and joy again. That is my hope for you.

Adapted from Public Access Internet Source[2]

Helpful Websites To Access Information About Suicide[1]

American Association of Suicidology: www.suicidology.org.

American Foundation for Suicide Prevention: www.afsp.org. The American Foundation for Suicide Prevention (AFSP) has compiled a national directory of survivor support groups for families and friends of one who completed suicide. This directory is listed state by state.

Crisis, Grief & Healing: www.webhealing.com. This is a website to understand and honor the many different paths to healing strong emotions.

Griefnet: www.griefnet.org, an Internet community of persons dealing with grief, death and major loss.

Griefwork Center, Inc.: www.griefworkcenter.com is committed to providing the highest quality educational and professional training programs on crisis intervention, sudden loss, traumatic grief, suicide awareness, hospice care, and caregiver burnout prevention.

GROWW: www.groww.com, a site for many losses including suicide, featuring help, message boards and chats.

Eye on the Media: www.eyeonthemedia.net, rates media that portray acts of suicide.

Meeting of Hearts: www.meetingofhearts.com, grief and bereavement support for all who have lost a loved one.

National Directory of Support Groups: www.suicidology.org/survivors support, lists the individual support groups and how to contact them.

PBS Online: www.pbs.org/weblab/living, living with suicide, shared experiences of loss.

SAVE (Suicide Awareness Voices of Education): www.save.org. The mission of SAVE is to educate about suicide prevention and to speak for suicide survivors.

SPAN (Suicide Prevention Advocacy Network):www.spanusa.org.

The Compassionate Friends: www.compassionatefriends.org, is a national non-profit, self-help support organization that offers friendship and understanding to families who are grieving the death of a child of any age, from any cause.

W.M.S.O.S. (West Michigan SOS support group): www.angelfire .com /mi2/westmisos

Appendix B

The Five Stages Of Grief

Denial – You may find it hard to accept the death or loss, especially if it occurs suddenly. An emotional numbness may set in, lasting from hours to weeks.

Anger – You may feel angry and resentful toward what you see as the cause of your loss—another person, yourself or even God. Your feelings may also stem from a sense of helplessness.

Bargaining – You'll find yourself bargaining with God.

Depression – Signs include lack of energy, inability to concentrate, and withdrawal from people and activities.

Acceptance – Eventually you will accept that your life has changed drastically and will never be the same. That doesn't mean your life will never be good again. It just means it's changed. As a result, you will be changed, too.

Elisabeth Kübler-Ross[1]

Appendix C

Tips

On what to say to a person who is grieving[1]

I am here to support you.

Give a hug (if you and they are comfortable with that form of expression).

I am so sorry this happened to you.

I love your son (daughter, wife, husband). I remember the time when...

Tell your favorite stories about their loved one.

When you feel like talking, I'd like to listen.

Tell me what is happening with you.

It must be very hard for you to go through this.

Here is a book/article that was helpful to me in my loss.

The memorial service was such a great celebration of his/her life.

I'll pray for you and your loved one.

Here is a picture/letter of your loved one that I especially like.

How do you *really* feel?

Be in the moment with the ones who are grieving.

Keep conversations short when visiting (at funeral home, wake, etc.)

Ways to be helpful

Take action rather than waiting for them to call you.

Make a phone call to inquire how they are getting along.

Visit them (call first!). Take food to their home. Make the visit brief.

Send a card with a story about the deceased.

Take the children on outings.

Invite the family to your home for dinner (when they are ready).

Write in a letter some remembrances about the person who died.

Holidays, birthdays and anniversaries are difficult. Call them just to tell them you are thinking of them.

Give a person a frame for a picture of the deceased. (A friend gave me a frame with music notes on it. I still have Steve's picture in that frame).

If asked, help take care of the deceased's clothing and personal items.

Answer the phone (immediately after the death).

Make phone calls to notify friends of the family of the death.

Avoid these clichés

You're doing so well.

Others have lived through it.

How fortunate you have two other children.

I know just how you feel.

Be strong. You'll get over it...in time.

Time will take care of everything because time is a healer.

You're young. You'll get married again and have other children.

It is God's will.

Have faith. God will take care of your loved one.

He/she is in a far better place.

He/she looks so natural (in the casket).

Avoid telling them your problems at this time.

Appendix D

Helpful Hints

For you who are grieving[1]

1. Nurture yourself. Do whatever will help you relax so that you can fill your emotional and spiritual needs.

2. Take sufficient time off work to rest up.

3. Join a bereavement support group.

4. Get professional help when needed.

5. Allow yourself to cry and express anger.

6. Talk to a special friend.

7. Accept your loss and intend to heal.

8. Give yourself permission to face the pain.

9. Give yourself time to heal.

10. Forgive yourself for any guilt and pain you feel.

11. Remember, the choice of suicide was that of your loved one, not yours.

12. Setbacks may occur. Don't panic if you have a setback.

13. Plan special things to do on special occasions.

14. Talk to a "survivor" so you will know that you will survive.

15. Light a candle for your loved one on anniversary dates and birthdays while looking at pictures of them and playing music they loved.

16. Take life a day or an hour at a time.

Appendix E

If You Are Having Thoughts Of Suicide, Read This

If you are feeling hopeless or helpless and have thoughts of suicide, please read this. Are you having thoughts of ending your life? You must be hurting so badly that you just want those horrible feelings of pain and confusion in your mind to go away.

What are the problems that are impacting you at this time? Is there someone you could talk to that you trust? A friend, a relative, a minister/rabbi, a school buddy, a girl friend, your mom, your dad, your sister, or brother? It only takes one person to listen to help you find a new way to resolve each problem, one at a time. That way you won't feel overwhelmed and you can find some relief from those negative thoughts and feelings you're having at this time. You can call the suicide hotline 24-hours a day, and someone will listen and help if you are finding your situation intolerable.

"Did you know that a chemical imbalance in the brain could be the cause of depression? Depression can make you feel like you're not a worthy person, that you have no purpose. There is chemical help for depression. If you are on medication, maybe you need a change. Is there a possibility you are over medicated?"[1]

Think of the times you are busy and don't have thoughts of suicide. Remember that you have both good and bad days.

How will taking your own life help your condition?

Take a few moments to think about hope instead of hopelessness.

I know a person who tried to take her own life but she didn't succeed. She told me that if only someone she could talk to had been there, it would have helped her. She said, "I didn't really want to die; I just wanted the pain to go away." Usually a person who is suicidal has those feelings only for seconds or minutes then those feelings dissipate.

My friend, Amara, who has struggled with suicidal feelings since she was a young child, offers these solutions:

—Don't give in to the belief that no one could possibly understand what you are going through.

—Don't let feelings of shame over your thoughts of suicide prevent you from reaching out for help.

—Remember that hopelessness develops when you haven't been able to find the solution or the answers about how to heal your pain. The answers are out there. Keep searching and asking until you find someone to help you with those answers.

Please think about the following suggestions:

1. Ask for assistance.

2. Even if you don't know exactly what you want or need other people to do for you, talk with someone and tell them your story.

Appendix F

Tips For Obtaining Social Security Benefits And Mental Health Services

1. Make an appointment with a psychiatrist. An interview will be set up in which the psychiatrist will determine whether your loved one meets the Diagnostic Statistical Manual (DSM IV)[1] criteria for mental illness. If so, the psychiatrist will fill out paperwork stating the diagnosis and documentation for eligibility for disability benefits.

2. Go to the Social Security Office and fill out the paperwork for eligibility for Supplemental Security Income (SSI) and Social Security Disability Income (SSDI). Bring with you:
—letter from psychiatrist
—loved one's Social Security Number
—loved one's W2 form from last job
—information about his/her home, work history, and sources of financial support
—loved one's birth certificate or other proof of age and citizenship
—dates of any military service
—names, addresses and telephone numbers of doctors, hospitals, clinics and institutions where treatment has been received and dates of treatment.

3. Before applying for community mental health services, research state and county mental health services. (We moved to the county that had the best program).

4. Make an appointment with a team manager. Bring with you:
—documentation from loved one's hospitalizations (three hospitalizations were required in Michigan for eligibility for mental health services)
—letter from psychiatrist
—loved one's Social Security Number
—loved one's W2 form from last job
—loved one's birth certificate
—loved one to be interviewed.
When all paperwork and interview is completed, you will be notified whether your loved one has been accepted into the program. When accepted into the County Community Mental Health Program, this is what to expect:
—a case manager will be assigned to your loved one
—a psychiatrist working for the mental health system will be assigned to your loved one
—he is responsible for prescribing medication
—team meetings every week, which you are welcome to attend
—questions you have for the case manager.

The case manager's job includes:
—dispensing and monitoring medications
—helping your loved one with finances, medication, daily living skills, employment, housing, shopping for food, personal needs, etc.
—visiting your loved one once or twice a week
—making recommendations to the team as to any changes that occur
—documenting all contacts with your loved one.

Based on guidelines for the state of Michigan[2]

Appendix G

For Lobbying Efforts

Here are a dozen reasons why you should sign an advocacy letter:[1]

1. Many suicides are preventable, if people get the appropriate treatment.

2. Every person who feels suicidal deserves treatment.

3. Every 41 seconds someone in this country attempts suicide.

4. Every 16.7 minutes, someone completes suicide.

5. Over 85 people a day die by suicide.

6. People can do something about suicide. They can exercise their First Amendment Rights by petitioning the government for change.

7. Yearly, at least 750,000 productive years of life (under age 65) are lost to suicide.

8. Many millions of hours are spent by survivors trying to cope with their losses.

9. Suicide is the eighth leading cause of all deaths, third in age group 15-24.

10. In the last 40 years, the suicide rate in 15-19 year olds has quadrupled.

11. Suicide causes are multifaceted: biological, sociological, psychological and societal.

12. The development and implementation of a National Suicide Prevention Strategy is dependent on *your* advocacy!

All district contact information can be obtained by going to www.congress.org. Information about how to contact members of Congress in their Capitol Hill offices can be obtained by calling 202-224-3121 or by going to "Write to Congress" on the NAMI Web site at: http://www.nami.org/policy.htm.

Sample letter[2]

Senate Adds Funding for Federal Mental Health Courts Program
Your advocacy is needed to keep this money in the final House-Senate
Conference report.

Date _____

The Honorable _____
U.S. Senator
Washington, D.C. 20510

Dear Senator:
    I petition you to please:
    Direct adequate resources to implement full funding for the new fed-
eral Mental Health Courts program as part of the FY 2002 Commerce-
Justice-State Appropriations bill (S 1215/HR2500). Mental health
courts have proven effective in curbing the growing trend of "criminalization" of mental illness by giving courts and prosecutors the tools
needed to divert offenders with severe mental illnesses into treatment
programs, rather than jails. It is unconscionable that people with severe
mental illnesses—legitimate medical conditions—who are not able to
access appropriate treatment, are being imprisoned.
    In 2002, Congress took a major step forward in helping courts and
criminal justice systems at the state and local level to provide access to appropriate treatment and services in the community for non-violent offenders when it passed P.L. 106-515. Now it must follow through and
provide full funding in FY 2002.
    Promote continuing judicial supervision over offenders with mental
illness who are charged with non-violent offenses, and endorse coordi-
nated delivery of services including specialized training of law enforce-
ment and judicial personnel to identify and address the unique needs of
offenders with mental illness.
    Please give serious consideration to this bill dealing with mental health
courts and the criminalization of people with mental illness.
    Thank you

Name_____
Street Adress _____
City_____State_____Zip_____
Signaure_____

Notes

Chapter 1: My broken heart
1. Ernest Holmes, "This thing called you" in *Science of Mind*, vol. 75, no. 19, p. 40 (October 2002).

Chapter 2: Family portraits
1. Shanta K. Hartzel, *Angel messages* (Elan Press: Boulder, CO, 1997), 19.

Chapter 4: Carl's incredible courage
1. Leo Busgaglia, Felice Foundation, P.O. Box 599, Glenbrook, NV 89413

Chapter 5: The journey after suicide
1. E. Kubler-Ross, *On death and dying* (New York: Simon and Schuster, 1997).
2. Website: www.spanusa.org (source: National Vital Statistics Report 50, 15, final data for 2000).
3. *Webster's New World Dictionary* (New York: Pocket Books Division, Simon & Schuster, 1995).
4. M. Williamson, *Illuminata* (New York: Random House, Inc., 1994), 30.
5. Henri Nouwen, *Wounded healer* (New York: Doubleday/Image, 1992), 12.
6. R. Camp, *Love cards* (Naperville, IL: Sourcebooks, 1997), 353.
7. A *Course in Miracles,* Foundation for Inner Peace, P.O. Box 1104, Glen Ellen, California 95442, Text.
8. Mitsuo Aoki, Seminar at Association of Unity Churches 2000 Convention, Honolulu, HI, June 6, 2000.
9. Leo Busgaglia, Felice Foundation. P.O. Box 599, Glenbrook, NV 89413.

Chapter 6: Dealing with the mental health system
1. Lloyd Siegel, *The New York Times*, 1981.
2. E.F. Torrey, *Surviving schizophrenia, a family manual* (New York: Harper & Row, revised edition 1988) p. xv.
3. Website: mental wellness.com (Schizophrenia and basic information, Reference Room Internet Source).

4. Ibid

5. E.F. Torrey, *Surviving schizophrenia, a family manual* (New York: Harper & Row, 1972).

6. E.F. Torrey, *Surviving schizophrenia, a family manual* (New York: Harper & Row, revised edition 1988), 3.

7. *Physician's Desk Reference, 56th Edition* (Montvale, NJ: Medical Economics Company, Inc, 2002).

8. C. Rees, *The alliance for the mentally ill* (Arlington, VA: National Alliance for Mental Illness, 1988).

9. *Your rights when receiving mental health services in Michigan* (Lansing, MI, MDCH, October 1997).

10. E. F. Torrey, *Out of the shadows* (New York: John Wiley & Sons, Inc., 1997).

11. National Alliance for Mental Illness, Arlington, VA 22201.

12. R. Carter, *Helping someone with mental illness* (New York: Times Books, 1998), 22.

13. *Putting People First*, President's Commission on Employment of People with Disabilities and Guidelines to Reporting and Writing About People With Disabilities, 3rd edition.

14. E. F. Torrey, *Out of the shadows* (New York: John Wiley & Sons, Inc., 1997), 186.

15. T. Gore, *Women & mental health*, interview with Tipper Gore (2001), Internet source: www.pbs.org/ttc/hottopics/ tippergore.html.

16. E. F. Torrey, *Out of the shadows* (New York: John Wiley & Sons, Inc., 1997), 187.

Chapter 7: My path back from tragedy

1. David Walker, *Science of Mind*, vol. 75, no. 19, p. 65 (October 2002)

2. G. Jampolsky, *Love is letting go of fear* (Berkeley, CA: Celestial Arts, 1979), 2.

3. D.N. Walsch, *Friendship with God* (New York: G.P. Putnam's Sons, 1999), 219.

4. D. Stein, *Essential reiki: a complete guide to an ancient healing art* (1996), 8.

5. S. Smith, *The 4T prosperity program* (Carmel, CA: The 4T Publishing Co., 1998), 101.

6. P. Yogananda, *The divine romance* (Los Angeles: Self-Realization Fellowship, 1985), 136.

7. I. Bolton, adapted from "Though we meet as strangers, by our love we shall be known," an excerpt from *My son...my son...a guide to healing after death, loss, or suicide* (Atlanta: Bolton Press, distributed by The Link Counseling Center, 1983).

8. "The Rose," words and lyrics by Amanda McBroom.

Chapter 8: Healing the inner self

1. A quote from *Maya Angelou's poetry collection unabridged* (inspirational cards).

2. Public Access Internet Source.

Appendix A

1. West Michigan Survivors of Suicide Newsletter, Spring Issue, April 2001, Barb Patterson, editor.

Appendix B

1. E. Kübler-Ross, E. & D. Kessler, *Life Lessons* (New York: Scribner, 2000), 78.

Appendix C

1. Lois A. Bloom, *Mourning After Suicide* (New York: The Pilgrim Press, 1986).

Appendix D

1. Lois A. Bloom, *Mourning After Suicide* (New York: The Pilgrim Press, 1986), 21.

Appendix E

1. *Suicide, the Preventable Death*, Division of Continuing Education, Western Michigan University, Kalamazoo, June 25, 1987.

Appendix F

1. *Diagnostic and Statistical Manual of Mental Disorders, Fourth Edition* (DSM IV, American Psychiatric Press, 1994).

2. Your rights when receiving mental health services in Michigan (Lansing, MI, MDCH, October 1997).

Appendix G

1. Website: www.spanusa.org/advocacy.html, *A dozen reasons why you should sign an advocacy letter* (SPANUSA, Inc. 5034 Odins, Marietta, GA 30068).

2. Form adapted from SPAN USA (Suicide Prevention Advocacy Network, USA)

About The Author

Retired award-winning professor emeritus of music therapy, accomplished musician and inspirational speaker, and a member in Who's Who of American Women, Mary Scovel, M.M. was a major contributor to a textbook, Music Therapy for Adults with Mental Disorders: Theoretical Basis and Intervention, 2nd edition 2002.

Launching out in a new genre, Mary opens her heart and shares her deepest pain of the loss of two sons as composer of the music and lyrics to an inspiring song, "My Broken Heart." In this haunting song on her single CD Mary expresses her emotions to help people heal their grief.

Mary and her husband, Ward, live in Hilton Head Island, South Carolina. They have facilitated Survivor of Suicide groups in Michigan, Oklahoma, Arkansas, Hawaii and currently in South Carolina. They have two daughters and four grandchildren.

Visit the author's website at: www.surviving-suicide.com.